KU-749-831

Jalal al-Din Rumi

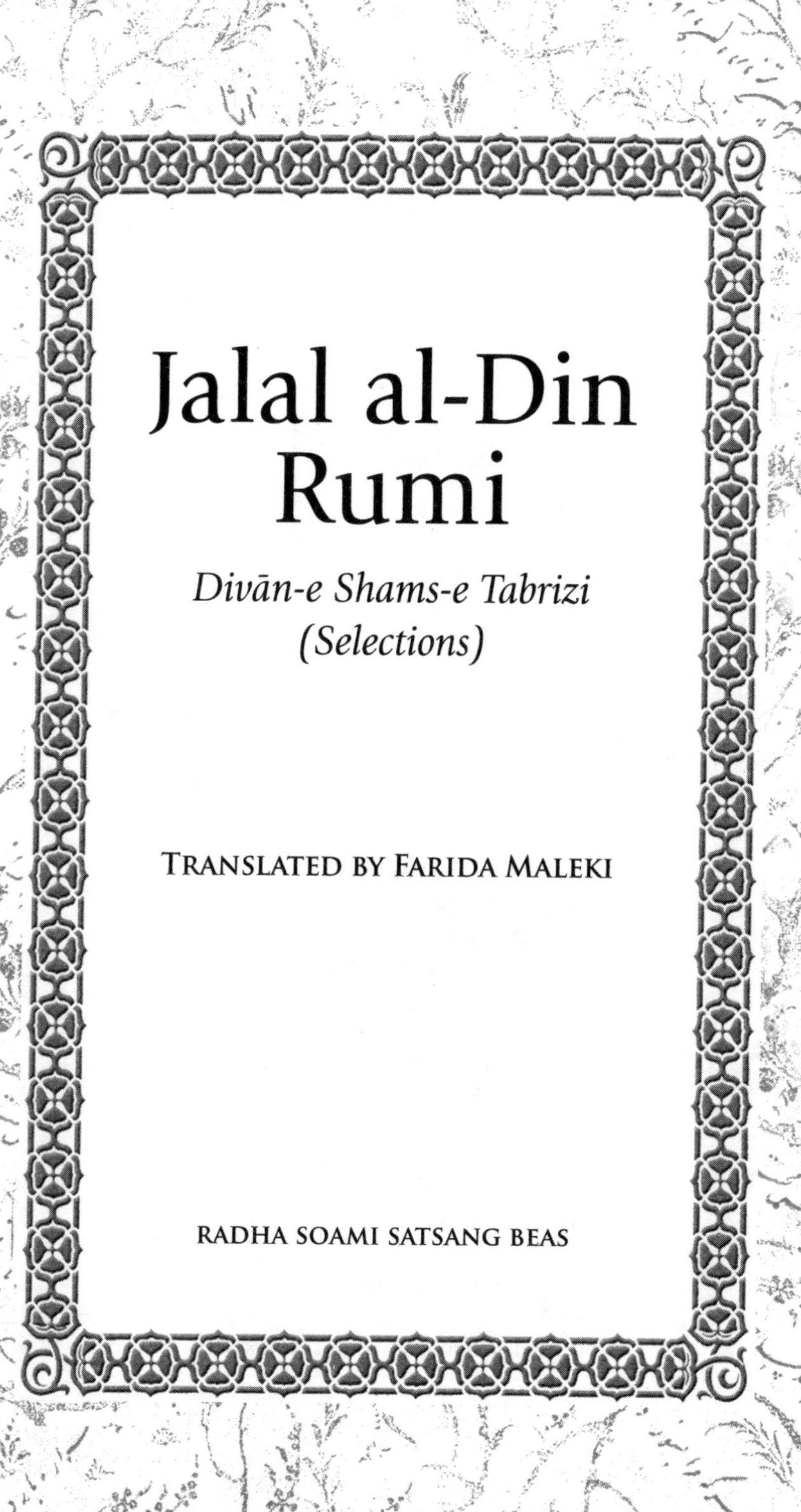

Jalal al-Din Rumi

Divān-e Shams-e Tabrizi
(Selections)

TRANSLATED BY FARIDA MALEKI

RADHA SOAMI SATSANG BEAS

Published by:
J. C. Sethi, Secretary
Radha Soami Satsang Beas
Dera Baba Jaimal Singh
Punjab 143 204, India

First edition 2019

24 23 22 21 20 19 8 7 6 5 4 3 2 1

ISBN 978-93-88733-18-2

Printed in India by: Gopsons Papers Ltd.

CONTENTS

NOTE FROM THE PUBLISHER

Transliteration provided in this book is an approximation of the Arabic and Persian pronunciation. RSSB publications use simplified transliteration for easier reading in preference to a more academic style. Readers are advised to refer to the original script or to an Arabic or Farsi language expert for exact pronunciation. Muslim names and Islamic terms in this book have also been simplified, leaving out some diacritical marks.

PREFACE

We are pleased to present *Jalal al-Din Rumi: Divān-e Shams-e Tabrizi (Selections)* in our Mystic Tradition series which portrays the lives and teachings of various mystics. The basis of our book, the *Divān* is one of Rumi's great works, born of the pain of separation from Shams – his beloved teacher and spiritual guide. The poems have been translated into modern English by Ms Farida Maleki, an Iranian American, from the compilation of the original thirteenth-century Farsi manuscripts by Badi' al-Zamān Furūzānfar.

Given the enthusiasm with which the publishing industry has produced books on Rumi's poetry in the last two decades, it is important to ask whether we need another. We feel the need for the present version because much of what has already been embraced as Rumi's poetry is incomplete, uses somewhat archaic language, or lacks many of the nuances that lie at the heart of Rumi's mystical teaching.

After Shams left him for the second and final time, Rumi composed more than 44,000 lines of poetry – an outpouring of love and longing of a disciple for his Master. Anyone who is fortunate enough to experience the love of a spiritual Master, or even the yearning for one, will certainly understand what is being presented here. But Rumi's work is not all about the pain of separation: there is joy, humour, instruction, withering sarcasm, reprimand – and, above all, love.

The poems are presented in Furūzānfar's original order for ease of reference, with a title we chose for each poem that emerged from the verses themselves. The brief description that accompanies each poem contains some piece of history or mythology or a specific explanation of an idea or term that helps understanding. Each poem "asked for" its own supplemental material and, in some cases, returning to the original Persian source revealed additional contextual material. Appreciating its essence, we did not avoid intricate mystical and esoteric content. The glossary and footnotes are also designed to help in understanding the poetry's context, references, and intrinsic meanings.

No attempt has been made to deconstruct the poems to the extent that they lose their original meaning. We have not romanticised Rumi nor softened the impact of his messages. In spite of the challenges presented by some unusual and obsolete language, the translations in this book remain as true to the original Persian language as possible. Some poems will be immediately understandable while others may require a more intense study to understand. However, their essence will be revealed over repeated readings. Each one is worth our time and attention.

We hope this book provides a source of inspiration to all seekers on a spiritual path. Here, Rumi gives us an understanding of separation and a hope for union as well as the invaluable insight that without separation, there can be no union.

J. C. Sethi
RSSB Publications
Beas, India

FOREWORD

With the grace of Allah, everything that is touched in the name of one of His greatest lovers, Maulana Jalal al-Din Rumi, turns to gold. With the glow of the golden light of the sun falling on people – their hearts, their intentions, their efforts – all begin to glow with Allah's grace.

I have been experiencing this wonder ever since I entered the world of Rumi and realised that what he said was all in the heart. I have watched the open-hearted, swept away by his love, their hearts on fire, their lives transformed. How fortunate I was to have encountered Rumi at a time in life when I still had many years ahead of me and was ready to benefit from – and share – his divine insight and wisdom. I was in Kashmir in 1988 making a film about the Kashmiri poetess Habba Khatūn when outside events forced a halt in production. Being left with a void of time to fill, I began reading a copy of Kabir Helminski's *Ruins of the Heart*, lent to me by a friend who knew of my growing interest in Sufi mysticism. It felt like immersion into a whole new world, a world in which, like the last line in one of Rumi's poems, "An unaccountable grace has come to you." I was smitten. Once I had been drawn into his orbit, Rumi became for me a dazzling comet which burned deeply into my spiritual horizons, sharpened my perception, and settled permanently into my heart.

Rumi has affected the tame and the wild, the sage and the child – and everyone who falls anywhere within these two extremes. Now, five centuries after Akbar cried while listening to Rumi's poetry, interest in the poet, his poetry, and his message only grows. And Rumi has enormous relevance today as a bridge between cultures. My friend Karan Singh, Chairman of the Rumi Foundation, says it well: "Rumi is the perfect antidote to our times, cutting across religious divide. He is the soft face of Islam: about love, humanism, and compassion."

In the eyes of Allah, all are the same – no matter how you address Him or spell his name – or for that matter, His messengers: Moses and Musa, Joseph or Yūsuf, Muhammad or Mehmet. Or even Rumi who is spelt as Celaleddin in Turkish and Jalaluddin in English and addressed as Molānā by Persians, Mevlana by Turks and Maulana by others, including Indians. The people of Afghanistan also add Balkhī before Rumi, as he hailed from Balkh.

Rumi's name may change but his appeal to the heart does not. And it's no wonder. Rumi himself keeps lifting you higher and higher through his philosophy and poetry, themes and symbolism, and through his piety and poverty. He continues to position you between what the world is thirsty for and what organized religion offers. His writings can touch you and transform you at any level: cerebral, emotional, ecstatic, or spiritual. And, if you pay attention, you will see that he is inviting us all on a journey, full of mysteries and wonders.

Human lives are quite mundane and simple, filled with anguish and frustration, and a deep sense of loss as time flies. A concern for the human predicament and the human race, for aesthetics and the finer values of life, and faith in the communication arts have all been central drivers of both my personal outlook and my professional life. I have always been passionate about sharing ideas with people. This new book on Rumi will be a valuable gift to readers who are already Rumi enthusiasts. And for those new seekers who are looking for a challenge or for a kindred soul, or seeking a path out of orthodoxy into a different Truth, Rumi can provide all that.

Rumi, the greatest poet of all times, did not want to be a poet, but a lover – he wanted to annihilate himself in the Beloved. Everything he wrote, everything he was, had one purpose – to pay passionate tribute to the Beloved. As he says in the *Masnavi*:

> The beloved is all that lives –
> the lover is a dead thing.[1]

So, I extend a sincere welcome to this new book of selections from the *Divān-e Shams-e Tabrizi* and anticipate that it will provide spiritual companionship for a caravan of new readers who will join with us in knocking at Rumi's door:

> With eyes closed, you ask,
> "Where has the bright day gone?"
> Then the sun hits your eyes, saying,
> "Here I am – open the door!"[2]

Muzaffar Ali
Secretary & Executive Director
Rumi Foundation
New Delhi, India
Summer 2018

Part One: INTRODUCTION

ABOUT THE BOOK

Everyone and everything perishes,
but celebration in your state of oneness
is forever, forever, forever.[3]

Today, more than seven hundred years after he composed his works, Jalal al-Din Muhammad Rumi – known affectionately simply as Rumi – is the world's most recognized and revered poet. A thirteenth-century Sufi mystic, Rumi has become a twenty-first-century bestselling author. Although misquoted nearly as often as he is quoted, Rumi is universally considered a poet of love, his words giving shape to the ache of longing, the pain of separation, and the ecstasy of union with the beloved. For Rumi, the path to the divine transcended creed and was accessible to any lover, regardless of culture or social order. "My religion," he wrote, "is love."[4] This message has resounded like a heartbeat through the centuries, appealing to today's seekers of love from all walks of life, much as it did in Rumi's own time.

Rumi, a highly educated and respected religious scholar, Islamic jurist, and Muslim preacher, was in his late thirties before he ever composed a line of poetry. It was then that he met Shams-e Tabrizi and verse began to pour from him. The selections in this book are taken from that fount, the *Divān-e Shams-e Tabrizi,* where more than 44,000 lines of poetry, dictated or sung by Rumi, capture the love between Rumi, the student, and his teacher Shams-e Tabrizi, the anguish of estrangement, and the journey to union with the beloved.

Nearly three thousand of those lines were chosen for their elegance, their imagery, and their focus on the spiritual path, as well as the inner practice of meditation, the importance of a living teacher, and the responsibilities of the disciple in a spiritual relationship. Many of these verses have been translated into English for the first time. Some better-known verses are included because they were simply too beautiful or too profound to ignore. The brilliance of his work and the universality of its message of love explain Rumi's enduring legacy and the ubiquity of quotations from his poetry.

For ease of reading, we have organized this book into two parts. The Introduction, Part One, contains this chapter on the source material, the method of translation, and some of the intricacies and highlights of Rumi's language and a second chapter with a short biography of Rumi. Part Two: Poetry presents 161 selections from the *Divān-e Shams-e Tabrizi.*

SOURCE MATERIAL

The poems in this book were chosen from the Persian edition of the *Divān-e Shams-e Tabrizi* compiled over a period of nine years (from 1957 to 1966) by Badi' al-Zamān Furūzānfar. A renowned scholar of Persian literature and Iranian linguistics and an expert on Rumi, Furūzānfar based his work on a comparison of nine older manuscripts and three newer, published editions of the *Divān*. He gathered and edited Rumi's poetry into ten volumes, two of which provide an index to facilitate searches for specific lines or poems and supply meanings for obscure or unusual words found in the poetry. This has been an invaluable resource for the translations presented here.

Although Rumi's language is simple, translation can be difficult due to his occasional use of archaic words that are either uncommon or entirely out of use in Farsi today and, additionally, to the disorganized order of stanzas or misspelled words which Furūzānfar painstakingly remedied. These errors occurred largely because the original *Divān* was destroyed in a fire in Konya, Turkey and had to be recreated from various manuscripts of Rumi's poetry. This loss and restoration may have impacted the integrity of the original line order in some poems.

To support our introduction to this collection of Rumi's poetry, we have translated and quoted details of Rumi's life and writings from another of Furūzānfar's books, *Treatise on Research on the Conditions of Rumi's Character and Life.*[5] In that volume, he authenticates dates and other historical and biographical information by comparing works from prominent early historians with three valuable primary sources on Rumi – two of which were written by those who actually knew Rumi and the third by a disciple of Rumi's near and dear grandson.

This work contains direct translations from the Persian of these three original sources:

- *Valad Nāmeh* is a book of poetry by Rumi's son, Bahā al-Din Sultān-e Valad, who lived in Konya all his life and was a disciple of Rumi's first teacher, Seyyed Borhān al-Din Mohaghegh-e Termezi, and then became a disciple of Shams-e Tabrizi. Ultimately, Bahā (who was also called Sultan Valad) became Rumi's second successor. His book was written eighteen years after Rumi's death.
- *Resāleh dar Manāgheb-e Khodāvandegār* is an account from one of Rumi's leading disciples, Faridūn Ahmad-e Sepahsālār, written at the request of someone the author calls "a close companion and partner in secrets." Though

the date of his manuscript is unknown, we know Sepahsālār to be a contemporary of Rumi's son, Bahā, and probably about the same age. This comprehensive volume describes Rumi's life and the lives of his father and family, *murshids** (teachers), successors, chief disciples, and sheikhs.

- *Manāgheb al-Ārefeen* is a two-volume book by Shams al-Din Ahmad Aflāki, a disciple of Rumi's grandson and third successor, Chelebi Jalal al-Din Āref. Written forty-six years after Rumi's death at the request of Āref, this manuscript includes Rumi's family tree and biographies of Rumi and his father, his *murshids* and nine family members, who also became *murshids*.

These works provide sources that are close enough to Rumi's life for us to move away from speculation and folklore to something that is closer to reality.

Finally, the prose contains original translations from Rumi's *Masnavi,* his epic book of spiritual teachings in poetry; excerpts from *Fih-e māfih,* Rumi's spiritual discourses; and translations from Brad Gooch's book, *Rumi's Secret.* We are also grateful for the meticulous research of Franklin Lewis and Mostafa Vaziri and the inspiring words from the contemporary Persian Rumi scholar, Dr. Mohammad Ali Movahed.

THE TRANSLATION PROCESS

The translation occurred in stages over the course of several years with a small multi-lingual, multi-cultural group. We first attempted to capture something close to a literal meaning, always bearing in mind that although there is often an appropriate single word in one language to match a single word in another, it is seldom the case that all the resonances, all the variations, all the connotations, and the

* See the glossary for full descriptions of foreign terms.

boundaries around the word will map exactly from one language to another. We are fortunate with English because centuries of borrowing from other languages – and a packrat capacity to store and use those words – provides us with a wide word palette from which to choose. In these translations, we attempted to reach for concepts that are compatible with the source and not just for the literal meanings of the words.

The translations were then recreated with a more poetic structure, seeking rhythm, repetition, alliteration, and word play consistent with the original – but seldom seeking to replicate the rhyme scheme. Not only have modern readers lost the capacity to be comfortable with rhyme in English poetry, but the end result often feels contrived and artificial. Nonetheless, we have often mapped other aspects of the Persian language structure into English, using repeated line endings and other lyrical elements.

The metaphorical web so well honed by the Sufis, and Rumi's extensive use of the Koran, hadiths,* and certain Persian cultural references, required us to write brief commentaries for each ghazal. To foster understanding, these commentaries offer snippets of the context in which the piece was written – by relating a relevant story; providing some sliver of meaning, historical setting, or religious background; or by highlighting some other point that adds depth. In addition, the subject index sheds light on other aspects of the poems to help readers with new or unfamiliar concepts and references.

We have generally capitalized words that refer specifically to God and placed all quotations from the Koran and all hadiths within single quotation marks. Explicit citations are in the footnotes that accompany the poems, but there are other hints and echoes of the Koran that have not been noted. Our objective was to provide informative supporting material without detracting from the beauty of the poetry itself.

---

* Sayings largely of the Prophet Muhammad, for a long time transmitted orally.

THE POETRY

The poetic form used by Rumi in this collection is the *ghazal*, a sophisticated and demanding type of verse embraced by medieval Persian poets to convey the pain of separation from the beloved as well as the joy of love. A ghazal is composed of five to fifteen verses and employs an intricate rhyme scheme, metre, and rhythm that enhance its musicality. Each verse has an ending refrain of one to three words (*radīf*) that repeat, preceded by an inline rhyming word (*qafia*). Though thematically linked, each verse in a ghazal is grammatically and syntactically complete, like pearls within a strand. The final verse of a ghazal includes the signature of the poet (*takhallus*), the author's name in either first or third person. In one interpretation, the *takhallus* can be seen as the clasp that fastens together the string of ghazals. Rumi periodically uses the signature of Shams in this final verse as if Shams himself were the author. Indeed, Rumi titled this monumental work, which translates as "The Collected Poetry of Shams-e Tabrizi," to make clear that his beloved teacher and spiritual guide was speaking through him. As he says:

> You took abode in my heart and soul – finally
> and made them both crazy – finally...
> O heart, I was trying to keep you busy
> but you remembered that fairy tale – finally...
> Shams-e Tabrizi, you made every particle
> wise and luminous – finally![6]
>
> Who am I to compose poetry?
> But that Turk inspires me.
> He comes and says, "Who are you then?"[7]

However, Rumi also closed several ghazals with *Bas!* (Enough! or Stop!) or with *Khāmūsh!* (Silence!), in a sense the signature of the inexpressible – specifically, the truth that cannot be known or expressed through words but that must be experienced. Rumi's call for silence in these ghazals also indicates that he cannot reveal any further inner secrets:

> Be silent, my tongue, since my heart is burning,
> your heart will burn, too, if I speak of my burning heart.[8]

> Silence! If I tell you about all his subtle points,
> you will break out of yourself.
> You will lose your roof and door![9]

And yet it was Shams whom Rumi invoked most often in his poetry, ultimately naming his beloved teacher in almost one thousand poems. Rumi was consistently and deeply humble when it came to his own poetry, attributing all the beauty that shone through his work to the grace of his beloved:

> Look! Without words,
> what is this talk in the heart?
> It's a colourless colour and a formless form
> rising from the essence.
> Shams-e Tabrizi is seated as king.
> Before him, my verses line up like chosen slaves.[10]

The verses are Rumi channeling Shams, multilayered, mysterious, and sometimes puzzling. Both Rumi and Shams took every opportunity to enrich their teachings, even single words and lines, with multiple images, multiple meanings, and multiple themes.

It is worth keeping in mind that Rumi, a Sufi mystic, used veiled and allegorical language. He wrote these poems nearly eight hundred years ago, and language changes over time. He was Persian by culture, which introduces subtleties, nuances, and even frank dissonances that we may miss. He was a scholar and teacher by profession; hence, he teaches us in these selections. He was Muslim by religion. He was a jurist of the Hanafi school, one of the four major schools of Islamic law, and highly educated in that field. He knew Arabic well. Muhammad and the Koran were central to his teaching; hence, we can understand his extensive use of Koranic verses and hadiths. By employing these scriptures, he taught spirituality through a familiar and revered medium and, simultaneously, taught the deeper, hidden meanings of the Koran. Indeed, his epic work, the *Masnavi*, was sometimes called the "Persian Koran" in his lifetime.

There is extraordinary beauty in Rumi's ghazals; we attempted to capture this beauty in our transition to English. The tone of the poems varies in many ways: devotional and didactic; joyous and sorrowful; serene and agitated; solemn and light. Accordingly, we varied the tone of our language to match the originals. For instance, in seeking to differentiate the lighter from the more solemn, we have echoed Rumi's own use of informal versus formal language.

In Rumi's poems, there is sometimes an exchange of voices that is regular and clear. Sometimes the pattern of voices and the identity of the speakers are more ambiguous or shift from one to another; then readers must work harder to be sure who is speaking.

In many cultures, the structure of a poem is linear: it has a beginning, a middle, and an end, and it often moves forward through time. The ghazals of the Persian poets – and Rumi is a quintessential Persian poet – are different. They are often comprised of a cloud of verses clustered around a topic, an idea, or a theme, hanging in space and time in a way that almost invites us to walk around it and view it in three dimensions. There are some parallels with the differences between traditional eastern and western classical music. In western music, we hear the statement of a theme, the development of that theme in a series of definable, sometimes quite formal ways, and then perhaps a second theme and, later, the restatement of the first theme – and so on. In music in the eastern traditions, the conventions are different with, again, some greater sense of the music hanging in space and time rather than moving through space and time.

There may be a verse in a ghazal that is difficult to understand because of the concepts under discussion, a cultural or historical reference, or its source in the Koran or a hadith. Understandably, some translators have decided to leave these lines out, but we have not, preferring to present complete ghazals. These are not necessarily easy poems to understand but neither is the spiritual journey they describe. Both demand our attention and effort. The veiled language, the metaphors, and the images can hide some facets of the poem while others are clear. Commentaries and introductory material that accompany the poems are intended to cast light on their hidden meanings. Footnotes and ancillary material in the glossary and appendixes provide additional support for interpreting the poems, but there will still be work for you to do. We made no attempt to dissect the poems so thoroughly that all is revealed. Instead, they will reveal themselves to you slowly over time as you return to them again and again.

RUMI'S LANGUAGE

To get the most out of the poems in the *Divān-e Shams-e Tabrizi*, it helps to understand that the entire work is a timeless love song to Shams: it expresses devotion to him, love and longing for him, and the pain of separation from him.

Second, because the language sometimes feels distant and inaccessible, when reading Rumi's ghazals it also helps to keep in mind how he uses language and how everyday physical and emotional phenomena can carry esoteric or mystical meaning.

Finally, there are other recurring themes layered into the text that give us additional insight into what compelled Rumi to spend so many years composing, reciting, and singing this poetry – in his meditation, while going about his everyday activities, during visits by community and religious leaders, and even on his deathbed.

In this particular translation, we have tried to walk a fine line between maintaining the integrity of a literal translation and capturing the intent, the rhythm, the repetition, and the musicality of the original. In some cases, we have left the original Persian word in the poetry where a comparable English equivalent does not exist. Two examples are *faqr* and *samā*.

Faqr, or humility, is an important Sufi doctrine and one of Rumi's favourite topics of discussion. *Faqr* literally means poverty but, for Sufis, it means the total destruction of human ego, the obliteration of duality. This realization is a fundamental requirement for treading the spiritual path. Only when the ego is fully annihilated is God automatically confirmed as the one, true, everlasting existence. When a seeker understands this truth, then he understands that everything, including his own self, belongs to God. He is just a beggar who possesses absolutely nothing. The experience of *faqr* brings about a profound sense of liberation and deep gratitude to God. Rumi describes this state:

> My heart and soul are free
> of themselves and from existence –
> they belong exclusively
> to the emperor of drunken souls.
> What an existence the soul found in non-existence!
> What a height the soul suddenly reached in this depth!
> When your love became a surgeon
> and opened my black dot,*
> I leapt out of myself and said, "What skill!"
> The physician of *faqr*
> jumped over and grabbed my ear, saying,
> "Good news, you are free from the pain of existence –

* The third eye.

free of waiting to see if the morning breeze will blow!
You are neither inferior to the sea
nor caught by a hook."
Buy and sell such goods from Shams-e Tabrizi
using his cache of wealth
from the bag tied to your waist.[11]

This multiplicity of meanings makes finding a single word to translate *faqr* essentially impossible.

Samā provides us with similar challenges. Literally, *samā* means "to listen," and in Sufi tradition it specifically refers to listening to devotional poetry. Often, it involves music; sometimes, movement and dance. Sufis believe that, by practising *samā* following proper instruction, the lover achieves expansion of the heart. This meditative practice is believed to have a variety of benefits because it removes the veils between the lover and beloved and allows the practitioner to turn away from the disappointment and anxiety formed by difficulty or failure on the spiritual path. It may deeply touch the soul and even shorten the journey to finding God. Rumi describes true *samā* this way:

That is not dancing, when every moment,
you're rising up like dust from the earth.
When you're rising, parting the two worlds,
ripping out your heart, and leaving your life –
that is dancing.[12]

Rumi devoted many lines of verse to *samā*, the practice that his beloved Shams had taught him and which he used to reach God:

Therefore, *samā* has become
the food and nourishment of the lovers of God,
because the gathering of the entire mind
focused on God is in it.[13]

TERMS OF ENDEARMENT

Essentially everything Rumi wrote was about Shams. In the poems in this book alone, terms of endearment and affectionate names for Shams occur well over one hundred times. It is not surprising to read about "the beloved" because we can relate to that term, even though we may hear romantic overtones. But we find Rumi giving Shams many other interesting names when he refers to him as "musician" or "minstrel" because he connects the soul of a lover with that divine inner music; "alchemy" because his very presence turns the base metal of the disciple's heart into gold; and "architect," "baker," or "cook" because he is the one who creates life's plans and delicacies. Rumi calls the inner presence of the teacher – and sometimes even Shams – the beloved, the friend, the king, the idol:

> O sweet-breathed minstrel,
> keep ringing your bell every moment.[14]

> More than once you promised to come,
> but it did not happen.
> O idol, this time, how have I found you?[15]

For Rumi, the sheikh is also the source of all sweetness. Rumi calls him the "sugar-pouring beauty," "quarry of sugar," and "the halva-selling friend, sweet as sugar." The sheikh is the king of lovers whom Rumi adorns with royal images such as Solomon, crowns, banners and belts.

Rumi calls him *Saqi,* the cupbearer, because the sheikh pours intoxicating bliss – divine love – from the jug of his own heart into the cup of the disciple's heart:

> O *Saqi,* intoxicate those who are proud
> of staying in their water and dust,
> so each will know how distant they have been
> from such a wealth as yours.[16]

O *Saqi,* swear that you will either
pour a cup of wine over the people
or call them to the height and breadth of love.[17]

METAPHORS, IMAGES, AND MOTIFS

Language is often used to hide rather than reveal the inner mystical path – which is certainly the case with Rumi's poetry. Over the centuries, Sufis have developed a coded language to communicate with one another to protect themselves from orthodox religious leaders. In this way, they also managed to avoid serious charges of heresy and, in some cases, a fate as extreme as a death sentence, not to mention lesser inconveniences. For example, consuming alcohol and drunkenness are forbidden in Islam, but Rumi's poetry is full of references to wine, drinking, and being drunk. This is Sufi coded language for intoxication with the inner sound and light. In Rumi's time, relating experiences of ecstatic absorption was more dangerous than physical drunkenness. Mansur al-Hallāj, a tenth-century Persian mystic, was hanged for proclaiming his oneness with God. Allusions to worldly intoxication brought only social stigma and disapproval:

Stroll through our town drunkenly
for, by order of our king,
both thief and guard are bound – bound.[18]

The king, Shams al-Din of Tabriz,
keeps me drunk, round after round.[19]

Sometimes Rumi drops the mask and lets us see through the metaphor of wine and drunkenness to the inner meaning:

Not drunkenness to make you desire sobriety,
but drunkenness that awakens your soul and wisdom.[20]

Rumi uses several repeating metaphors and motifs to describe the body, mind, and soul depending on the context of the individual ghazal. The house of water and dust or water and clay is the human body, into which the soul has been born:

> When I move from house to house,
> I am like a ray of sun.
> I am ruby, gold, and carnelian,
> born from water and clay.[21]

In relation to meditation, "house" refers to the body and "roof" to the head where the point of concentration can be found:

> Ten times you traversed the road to that house –
> for once, come up to the roof of this house.[22]

> I said, "Show me the ladder to climb to the sky."
> He said, "Your head is the ladder – just step on it!
> Put your foot on your head, step beyond the stars.
> Once you crush desire, come, step into the air!
> There, across the sky, a hundred paths will appear.
> Every dawn you will fly like a prayer to the sky."[23]

The mirror is a metaphor for the mind because it can reflect God's light with clarity, depending on its purity and proximity to God.

> Whenever the sun shines on the mirror,
> what can the mirror say but, "I am the sun?"[24]

The curl refers both to hair and to the rope by which the beauty of the beloved ensnares the disciple, and he uses the features of curls and ringlets as metaphors for the ups and downs of the world:

Oh, your lovely curls are the shackles around our necks.
The bird of my soul is nesting in those ringlets.[25]

Because the curl of your hair
is home and hearth for my mind,
only the form of a shadow
remains of my mind.[26]

Sufis cloak their meanings in other ways as well. Love for the spiritual master, of which Rumi's was boundless, is disguised as physical love. The human body is the house, and the soul is the hidden treasure within the house. In fact, the meanings can be so completely veiled that some Sufi teachers have written entire books for the sole purpose of explaining common metaphors and imagery.

This coded language includes a range of metaphors, similes, images, word use, and word play that fits within Sufi culture and resonates with their audience. Teachers who live by the sea or by the banks of great rivers use the image of crossing the water as a metaphor for the inner journey and the need for a captain who knows how to steer the boat; those who live in a trackless desert speak of the journey of the camel train and look to the leader to take them safely to the caravanserai to sleep for the night. Reducing the global to the local is exactly the same strategy that Jesus employed in his parables. Thus, Sufi teachers communicate their knowledge of the divine by using familiar words and images and by employing well-known stories from books that are still widely read, including the Torah and the Koran.

Some people delight in the ambiguity of the Sufi poems because they think that we can interpret these gems of mysticism in any way we desire. However, the ambiguity of Rumi is not the ambiguity of vagueness; rather, it is an ambiguity that comes from the multi-layered nature of the teachings of the mystics set against a backdrop of danger and threat of persecution. Many of these gloriously transcendent poems also impart practical advice about how to live daily life, how to meditate, how to control the mind, how to annihilate the ego, and how to achieve union with the inner Beloved, with God.

Rumi took lessons from his own teacher, Shams, who reminded us that understanding will come if we are patient and diligent:

> If you wait, both the answer and the one who gives the answer will come. Even if you do not get your answer, the meaning will come. The blessing of patience is that it gives power to the listener, offering extra help for the rest of his knowledge.[27]

This is certainly true of the poetry of his beloved disciple, Rumi.

IMAGES FROM THE NATURAL WORLD

Roses are a universal symbol of love and an offering of love. Sufis have often portrayed the rose as the beauty and perfection of the beloved, and the nightingale sings of its longing for a vision of the rose as a symbol of the intensity of the disciple's longing for union with the beloved. The rose garden is an inner level where the lover's heart opens, and a bouquet of roses is the evidence of spiritual achievement that the lover may offer the beloved:

> The rose garden of his face is the soul's grazing place.
> Ah – how the soul is nourished by that rose garden![28]

> … show me a bouquet of roses if you see that garden …[29]

The moon is a reference to the beloved's beauty and also to one of the lights on the inner path:

> Can the moon ever compare
> to the beauty of your face?[30]

If you look into murky water,
you see no moon, no sky.
The sun and the moon are hidden
when the air darkens.[31]

Rumi was a scholar in a variety of disciplines, not just law, as is obvious from his poetry and his discourses – and from some of the comments that both Shams and some of his contemporaries made about him. Drawing on his knowledge of astrology and astronomy, Rumi makes references to heavenly phenomena for word play, as metaphors for inner worlds, or just to describe the physical universe. He mentions the sun at least once in about every three ghazals, typically as a pun on Shams' name, which means "sun" in Arabic. He also refers to – and plays with – the states of matter (usually referred to as the five elements) of which living creatures are composed:

In the heavens, Jupiter beats his drum
to announce that love is coming.
A hundred blessings
for souls of lovers are coming.[32]

What is that Water that makes a lover,
full of wind and fire, so desirous
that he becomes like a carpet of dust on earth?[33]

Silver and gold can refer to the inner light or the Beloved – whom he also calls the Mine of Silver or the Mine – or to worldly wealth, depending on the context:

When the pure, silvery body hugs us tightly,
we will tame the restive colt that is the sky.[34]

If you scatter silver and gold for worldly profit,
you will not benefit unless you do this.[35]

Rumi also refers to the astrolabe, an instrument used to determine the positions of planets, as a metaphor to describe the need for a teacher on the spiritual path and the potential of the disciple to reach God:

> A human being is an astrolabe of God, but you need an astronomer to know how to use the astrolabe. If a seller of leeks or a greengrocer possessed an astrolabe, what would be the use? How could he fathom the conditions of the celestial spheres, or the turning of the houses of the zodiac, or their influences? Only in the hands of an astronomer is the astrolabe beneficial, for whoever knows himself knows his God.[36]

> The human being is an astrolabe of divine attributes.
> Adam's qualities manifest God's signs.
> What shows in him is His reflection,
> like the moon's reflection in the water of a stream.[37]

Rumi uses the image of an ocean to refer to God and, at other times, it can mean the ocean of existence that we must cross in order to obtain the inner treasure:

> Humankind, like waterfowl,
> is born from an ocean of souls.[38]

The word sugar is used to refer to the inner music:

> O sweet story-telling Sound of the flute,
> we taste the sugar in your Sound.[39]

> Hear my gratitude for Him –
> I swear upon your life and soul
> that I have never tasted sugar
> so sweet, so delightful![40]

BIBLICAL REFERENCES & STORIES FROM THE KORAN

In our collection of poems, there are more than ninety references to stories from the Bible and the Koran, or to a hadith. We must remember that Sufis practise and teach the mystic path that has its roots in Islam. In that culture, the Koran and Muhammad are central. Those of us who do not have any formal religious training or who have not read the Bible or the Koran may miss many of Rumi's references. Without this background, full understanding of the poetry is quite challenging. This is especially true when the poetry is rendered close to its original Persian form and retains its esoteric references.

Rumi's extensive use of Koranic verses and Biblical stories allows him to root difficult teachings in familiar stories until human understanding and inner capacities can catch up with the profundity of the teachings. Several poems in the *Divān* illustrate the difference in levels of spiritual attainment between teacher and disciple. They draw a contrast between the Beloved's power and purity and our absorption in the illusion that is our life:

> When you go just a little beyond yourself,
> past these skies, you will see
> the king of truth and meaning –
> and his banners and pavilions
> made of ancient light.[41]

Rumi also draws upon his knowledge of law and scripture to reinforce his points; for example, using the story of Joseph from the Judeo-Christian tradition gave him a way to mirror his own feelings of looking at Shams. The women who were cutting oranges were so distracted by Joseph's beauty that they cut their hands:

> O Soul, come to me,
> so my life stands front and centre,
> like the women who cut their hands
> in Joseph's presence.[42]

Or like Jacob, Joseph's father, forlorn because he is separated from his beloved son, Rumi longs only to see the Beloved:

> Like Jacob, I ceaselessly sigh in sorrow.
> The pleasure of seeing Joseph of Canaan
> is my desire.[43]

Muhammad (or Mustafā) is the ideal of the Sufi teacher, the captain of the caravan, depicted often by Rumi as the young, energetic, charismatic source of inspiration, teaching, and clear-headed leadership. He says:

> Fortune is on our side
> and our task is to give up life.
> Our caravan leader, Mustafā,
> is the pride of the world.[44]

Shams and Rumi, despite clearly separating themselves from the conventions of learned practitioners of Islamic law in which they were trained, insisted on conforming to the social and religious norms and obligations of Islam. Even enlightenment does not free one from the need to set an example for others. Shams says:

> Those who do not believe in attending to socio-religious acts are not worthy of being spiritual leaders, for spiritual leaders are the support and refuge of the entire world and its inhabitants.[45]

Both practised what they taught.

THE INNER MUSIC

Music is everywhere in Rumi's verse and was frequently a key element of *samā*. It is certain that much of his verse would have been sung, in the same way that the poetry of Guru Nanak, Mira Bai, and Sheikh Farid is sung in India. Music finds its way into the poetry itself, with ghazals that play on words like "mode" and "scale." Rumi's poetry in the Konya manuscript is ordered according to its metre, in a manner similar to the way that the Adi Granth is ordered by raga so that it is easier for the singer to know details such as the appropriate scale, rhythm, and musical motifs. The inner music is the very heart and substance of his ghazals, his teachings, and his life:

> This house – where the sound of the bell
> is constantly ringing – what kind of house is it?
> Ask the owner.[46]

> Hear the sound of His music played in my chest.
> My ruined heart begins to throb as it starts.[47]

Rumi calls the inner music the Water of Life or Wine:

> Don't give value to a life lived without love.
> Accept love – the Water of Life –
> into your heart and soul.[48]

> Before grapes, vineyards, or wine in the world,
> our soul was drunk on everlasting Wine.[49]

> Isn't my body a cup for that eternal Wine?[50]

And, as he does in the opening lines of the *Masnavi*, he refers in the ghazals to the reed and the flute:

> Oh, you have triumphed over the world!
> Sound of the flute, sound of the flute, sound of the flute.[51]

STYLE AND SUBSTANCE

Rumi's poetry in the *Divān* is the expression of his love for the divine, both in separation and in union. In many poems, Rumi teaches different aspects of the path, advising seekers by sketching his own experiences. There are also poems for those whom he loved dearly such as Sheikh Salāh al-Din and Hosām al-Din, poems for those who had offended him and were repeatedly expressing opposition to *samā*, and a few that mark specific occasions such as the marriage of his elder son or the birth of his first grandchild.

Although his language is heavily cloaked with metaphors, it is essential to remember that the primary purpose of his poetry is to speak clearly of the spiritual path. In Aflāki's *Feats of the Knowers of God* (*Manāgheb al-Ārefin*), we are offered a rationale for the style and substance of Rumi's writings:

> One day, while enthusiastically speaking about divine Truth and mysteries, Maulana Rumi said, "This country [speaking of Rum in present-day Turkey] is among the best of countries, but its people were unaware of God's realm of love and inner joy. God made cause from the causeless world and pulled us from the domain of Khorāsān to the country of Rum.... Because they had no inclination towards Haqq [Truth] and would remain deprived of divine mysteries, we presented those meanings to them through the gentleness of samā and poetry that is pleasing to people's nature. Because the people of Rum seek joy and pleasure as when a child becomes ill and hates the physician's drink but likes sweet fruit juice, the physician pours the medicine into fruit juice and gives it to the child so that he will drink it with pleasure and regain health."[52]

→→ ←←

There are as many preconceptions of what defines a spiritual teacher as there are spiritual teachers themselves. One generalization of such a guide is a distant, sombre figure who makes grand pronouncements about the road to God. For more than half his life, Rumi embodied that notion. He was serious and reserved in his youth and a scholarly, revered Islamic lawyer in adulthood. Rumi was a highly respected pillar of his society – until he met Shams. From then on, he was an intoxicated madman, drunk on divine love, from whom poetry flowed like a wild river of stars. Within that flow, Rumi describes the spiritual journey and shows us how to undertake it. Though the heart of his teachings is practical and resounds with the ultimate simplicity of truth, Rumi's words require effort to understand. Much like the journey to union with the divine itself, we must put in the work to achieve an understanding of Rumi. In order to find the treasure, we must know where to look. With the *Divān-e Shams-e Tabrizi,* Rumi points the way.

ABOUT RUMI

I am not this body lovers see,
I am that joy and happiness you feel within
when hearing my words or my name.[53]

For most of us, Rumi is a distant historical figure shrouded in mystery, who left behind an extraordinary body of luminous poetry filled with profound spiritual insight. He is referred to as a Sufi poet, a Muslim mystic, the spiritual leader and founder of the Mevlevi order, and more recently as a poet of divine love whose verses have been adapted to present him as a kind of New Age guru. Despite his nearly universal name-recognition, Rumi himself remains elusive, almost mythological, and often coloured by the perspectives of those describing him. However, through his early biographers, Sepahsālār and Aflāki, and his son Sultan Valad, we can see Rumi through a much more intimate, human lens and better understand the spiritual journey he shares with us through his verses. Here, we find the story of an intelligent, compassionate, and deeply loving man.

Although it is often misleading to view the past through modern eyes, there are some aspects of Rumi's life and character that stand out clearly across the centuries, regardless of the cultural or historical lens through which they are viewed. In a hierarchical society, Rumi, a learned and important public figure, felt at home with artisans and common working people. In an intensely religious Islamic community, he embraced people of all faiths. In a world strongly dominated by men, he accepted women into his assembly. In a society where women were mostly denied education, he taught girls to read and write. In the presence of strict rules and expectations about clothing and behaviour, he dressed as a wandering Sufi and danced in *samā*.

Rumi was austere and ascetic in the way he lived his own life, yet he did not judge the behaviour or transgressions of others. In an inflexible world, perhaps the only behaviour that could provoke his intolerance was intolerance itself. Even by today's standards, he was a surprisingly modern man. It is easy to understand why he was so deeply loved by his teacher, Shams, his disciples, and his community – and why he remains beloved today.

BEFORE SHAMS

Rumi's given name was Muhammad and, early on, his father called him Jalal al-Din (Glory of Religion). He was born into a highly regarded family on 30 September 1207 in Balkh, a city in the Persian state of Khorāsān, now in northern Afghanistan. Originally home to Zoroastrianism and, later, Buddhism, Balkh was well known by then as a centre of Islamic learning. Rumi's father, Mohammad ibn Hossein-e Khatibi, known as Bahā al-Din Valad or by his title, Sultan al-Ulamā (Sultan of Scholars), was a learned man, a Sufi master, and a religious lawyer.

Rumi was five years old when, according to Aflāki, he began having visions of angels that unsettled him. Rumi's father reassured his young son, telling him that the angels were offering gifts and blessings. At around this time, Bahā Valad left Balkh with 300 people[54] including family members, friends, and a group of his followers. Sepahsālār and Aflāki believe this migration was set into motion by personal conflict, but the close proximity of invading Mongol tribes was also a factor in the decision to leave. The intention of the group was probably to go on *Hajj** and then to find a new place to live.

Legend has it that along the way they met Farid al-Din 'Attār, the great Sufi author of *The Conference of the Birds*, who gave a copy of his *Book of Mysteries (Asrār Nāmeh)* to the young Rumi and predicted his future spiritual greatness. It is also said that when the family reached Damascus, Rumi and his father visited ibn 'Arabī, the most famous Arabian Sufi master. As they left, Rumi walked respectfully behind his father and 'Arabī commented, "Praise be to God! An ocean is moving behind a lake!"

Not long after they began their journey from Balkh, they learned that their former hometown had been destroyed and its inhabitants butchered by the army led by Genghis Khan. Though written accounts differ on the details of their journey, they eventually settled in Larandah, a city in Rum. It is this region that gave Rumi what is now his popular name, although no one ever called him that in his lifetime. Rum – the Persian and Turkish word for Roman – was originally part of the Byzantine Empire, the long-lived eastern remnant of the Roman Empire. In his time, Rumi was known and loved as Maulana Rumi, Master among the Romans.

At age eighteen, Rumi married Gowhar Khatūn. They had two sons: Bahā al-Din Muhammad Sultan Valad, named for his grandfather, and Alā al-Din. Sultan Valad became Rumi's second successor and biographer of both his father and grandfather. By the mid-1220s, the family was living in central Anatolia. Some time later, Rumi's father was summoned to Konya, now in Turkey, where he resumed his teaching and preaching under the patronage

* Pilgrimage taken by Muslims to the Kabah, in Mecca, Saudi Arabia.

of the Seljuk Prince, Ala' al-Din Kaikubad. The prince had built a mosque in Konya, surrounded himself with scholars and mystics from many places, and wanted to include Rumi's father in that esteemed group. The family moved into a madrasa built for them, which came to be known as the Madrasa Khudāvandegār, named after a respectful Persian word for lord or master. The madrasa was located near the markets, allowing artisans and merchants to easily hear his teachings, in addition to those from the elite classes. Bahā Valad's disciples, who included women, came from a variety of faiths and social strata. Rumi, his father's constant companion, would later attract an even more diverse group of disciples.

In 1231, just two years after the family had arrived, Rumi's father died. Rumi was twenty-four years old. Later, Sultan Valad would write that, after the funeral of Bahā Valad, "all the people, young and old, gathered around, and looked to his son, saying, 'You are like him in beauty. From now on we will hold onto the hem of your robe. We will follow you wherever you go. From now on you are our king.'"[55] Thereafter, Rumi occupied his father's seat in the mosque and began to give discourses.

THE NEED FOR A GUIDE

When Rumi's family was still in Balkh, his father entrusted Rumi's education to his own disciple, Seyyed* Borhān al-Din Mohaghegh-e Termezi. When the family left Balkh, Borhān went back to his birthplace, Termez. Borhān regularly inquired about Bahā Valad's whereabouts but did not reach Konya until a year after Rumi's father died. He sent word to Rumi, still grieving the death of his father, who was visiting Larandah, his former home and the place where his mother was buried. Upon receiving Borhān's letter, Rumi, who had not seen his first *murshid* for fifteen years, was filled with joy. Rumi wrote about Borhān:

---

* Descendant of the Prophet Muhammad's tribe.

Fortune's bower bears a gifted rose like you
but once each thousand years; not every age,
not each celestial house, brings forth a you.
Time bears a you to set the world in motion.[56]

By all accounts, Borhān was indeed a spiritually advanced Sufi. Aflāki writes about Borhān's spiritual gifts and the short time he took to achieve realization, "When he started on the spiritual path, the entire length of his ascetic discipline was only forty days."[57] Borhān was also a learned scholar and a noble and upright man. He had read many works of previous great masters and guided others on the inner path. Rumi says, "He had become the light, disregarded worldly appearances, and was intoxicated by Divine manifestation."[58]

Rumi, who was still too young to take up the full weight of his father's mantle with all of its duties, began training in Sufism under Borhān's guidance. A year later, Borhān sent him to Aleppo and then Damascus to complete his training. On this trip, Borhān accompanied Rumi as far as Kayseri, where he stayed while Rumi went on to Damascus. In those days, Aleppo and Damascus were among the most important centers of Islamic learning. As a result of the Mongol incursions in the region, many advanced, learned Persians, as well as many Sufis, appreciated the town's proximity to the sacred Mount Lebanon and had settled there. Rumi attended Halāviyyah, a highly regarded centre of Hanafi legal studies. He studied in Aleppo and Damascus for a total of seven years.[59]

Borhān al-Din formally initiated Rumi into the Sufi path when Rumi returned to Kayseri from Syria around 1237. Following Sufi tradition, Borhān trained Rumi in the practices of asceticism, especially periods of fasting, which Rumi would continue for the rest of his life. Fasting required discipline and the renunciation of worldly pleasures, and it increased the hunger for God.

Ramadan, the month of fasting for Muslims, became a time of joy for Rumi:

> Congratulations! The month of fasting is here!
> Have a good journey, my companion in fasting.
> I climbed to the roof, to see the moon,
> with my heart and soul, I longed for fasting.
> When I looked up, my hat fell off,
> my head was set spinning by the king of fasting![60]

After nine years as Rumi's teacher, Borhān considered Rumi's spiritual training to be complete, and he sent his student back to Konya to assume a position of leadership in his community. Borhān said, "Now you have all your father's virtues and are adorned with knowledge of God and knowledge of the world."[61]

Aflāki relates that on one occasion Borhān gave this advice: "First, eat only enough food to satisfy your hunger. Second, desire only enough clothing to cope with heat and cold, and third, wish for only enough respect in life so as not to be mocked by others."[62]

Soon afterward, Borhān died in Kayseri. At almost the same time, when Rumi was approaching his mid-thirties, Rumi's wife Gowhar Khatūn also died of unknown causes. Rumi had lost both his mentor and the mother of his sons within a short period of time, beginning to cut his links to the past. Rumi then married Kerra Khatūn, a widow. In time, Rumi and Kerra had two children: a son, Muzaffar al-Din Amir Ālem, and a daughter, Malekeh.

Following his father's tradition, some time after 1237 Rumi began to teach Islamic law and guide seekers of God, which he continued to do for approximately five years. He achieved great fame as an expert in Islamic law and great popularity as a speaker on Islamic spirituality. Like his father, he counted both women and men as his disciples. Aflāki says that Rumi held teaching positions at four separate madrasas. Rumi's discourses attracted followers from all walks of life, even those who did not understand their literal content. Rumi recalled:

> I was speaking one day to a crowd that included non-Muslims, and during my talk they were weeping and going into ecstatic states. "What do they understand? What do they know?" someone asked. "Not one out of a thousand Muslims can understand this sort of talk. What have they comprehended that they can weep so?" It was not necessary for them to understand the words. What they understood was the essence of the speech … the oneness of God.[63]

While generous with his time and teaching, Rumi was uncomfortable with fame and its trappings. Aflāki says one day Rumi told his disciples, "Since the day my fame grew, people have been coming to see me, and I haven't had any peace. But this is the Command, what can anyone do?" Rumi warned his followers about the troubles that come with fame:

> Make yourself deplorable and miserable,
> so it keeps you away from fame.
> To be famous among people is a strong rope.
> On the path it is as solid as iron chains.[64]

Aflāki says that Rumi often prayed for his disciples, saying, "For God's sake, remember companionship is very important and highly valued."[65] It was meaningful companionship that Rumi lacked as he entered his late thirties. He had achieved high standing in his community at a young age, amassed a sizeable and enthusiastic following, and lived a pious, spiritual life. Yet he had doubts about his own level of achievement and felt a lack of completeness. There was nobody – no friend or guide – from whom he could now learn more:

Because I am not from here,
I am a stranger here – a stranger.
Because I am restless here,
I must be from somewhere else![66]

Sultan Valad describes Rumi's profound understanding of his own need for a teacher. He notes that Rumi "was a highly educated and revered religious scholar and, at the same time, a follower of the Sufi path." Despite his own position and revered status, he "desired the priceless company of a saint and perfect Sheikh."[67] Rumi himself would later describe the longing of the heart for such a guide this way:

My ear awaits your message.
My soul longs, with life itself, for your greeting.
In my heart, the blood of yearning is boiling,
awaiting the scent of your bubbling wine cup.[68]

Anatolia became increasingly unstable in the 1230s, both because of internal strife among the ruling Seljuks and because of the looming presence of the Mongols from the east. Beginning in the 1240s, the Mongols made inroads into Anatolia either by direct conquest and pillage or because city rulers chose to surrender and become vassals. Konya was among the cities that began paying tribute and became one more Mongol territory. As the region and the city fell under the control of the invaders, Rumi's life changed dramatically and forever.

MEETING SHAMS

Shams al-Din Mohammad ebne-Malekdād-e Tabrizi, known as Shams-e Tabrizi, was a wandering Sufi and mystic iconoclast who had spent decades travelling from one religious capital to another, attending lectures by renowned teachers in search of a true saint.

Although he met several men whom he considered spiritually advanced, none passed his rigorous form of testing:

> Whomever I love, I oppress. If he accepts it, I roll up like a ball in his lap. Faithfulness is something that you practise with a five-year-old child, so he will believe in and like you. But the real thing is oppression.[69]

From his mid-forties, Shams, had desired the company of one of God's chosen souls, someone to be his companion and friend:

> I was told in a dream that I would be given the companionship of a saint. I asked where he was. The next night in my dream, I was told that he was in Rum. After some time, I was told, in another dream, that it was not yet time. "All affairs are subject to time."[70]

In 1228, during one of his stays in Damascus, Shams had seen Rumi, who was then studying Islamic law, and had attended Rumi's discourses. Though drawn to the young man, Shams knew Rumi was not yet ready to receive his spiritual guidance:*

> I was strongly attracted to you from the beginning, although when you began to speak, I could see you did not yet have the receptivity to understand these secrets. Had I told you then, it would not have been possible for you to comprehend them. This time would have been wasted ...[71]

Aflāki also mentions this encounter between Rumi and Shams in Damascus, which is related by the "ancient friends," meaning the old followers of Rumi, who depicted Shams in the midst of people as a "strange man ... with a black felt robe and a black hat.

* The *Maqālāt* contains four references to this fifteen or sixteen-year time lapse.

Maulana takes his hand and states, 'Purifier of the world, save me!' but Shams disappeared into the crowd."[72]

Shams was indeed an outlier – a stranger. Despite his enormous influence on Rumi, the very existence of Shams remained unverified to scholars until a collection of his teachings and discourses, the *Maqālāt-e Shams-e Tabrizi,* was found in the archives of a Turkish library in the mid-twentieth century. Before this discovery, some historians had decided that Shams was a figment of Rumi's imagination. In the *Masnavi,* Rumi says:

> No one is such a stranger in this world as Shams.[73]

Shams says of himself:

> If you have seen me, why do you still see yourself? If happiness is yours, how did you fall into unhappiness? If you are with me, how are you still with yourself? And if you are my friend, how are you still your own friend?[74]

On a clear November day in 1244, this stranger, Shams, arrived in Konya and stayed not in a Sufi lodge as would have been customary, but in a merchant inn disguised as a trader. Sixteen years after their first encounter, the student, Rumi, was ready. And so the teacher, Shams, appeared.

There are several miracle-decorated stories about this momentous meeting, all of which were written many years after the death of both, except for Sultan Valad's. Although we do not know the exact date of Sipahsālār's account, Aflāki's was written forty-six years after Rumi died. Some of these tales are not in harmony with Shams' own account. Even those of Sipahsālār and Aflāki differ widely. Although almost certainly embellished beyond credibility, these accounts demonstrate the awe-inspiring power of the meeting between Shams and Rumi.

One story has Rumi alone or sitting with his students with some books around him. Shams arrives and asks Rumi, "What are these books?" Rumi replies that Shams would not understand. Then, depending on the source, the books either catch fire or are thrown into the water. When Shams retrieves them, undamaged by the fire or water, Rumi asks, "What is this?" Shams replies that Rumi would not understand.

Aflāki gives another account:

> When Shams saw Maulana he asked him if Muhammad (Prophet of Islam) was higher in rank or Bāyazīd (a famous Sufi master). Maulana said, "What kind of question is this? Muhammad is the last prophet so where is the relevance?" Shams asked, "Then why did Muhammad say to God: 'We have not known you as befits you,' and Bāyazīd say: 'Praised be me; how grand my rank!'?" Maulana fell unconscious hearing this awe-provoking question; when he regained consciousness, he took Shams to his home and, for forty days, no one dared disturb their privacy.[75]

Sepahsālār gives the most likely account:

> Shams came to Konya in the cloak of a trader and rented a room in the rice-dealers' quarters, outside of which were small well-furnished chambers for meeting and socializing. One morning, Rumi approached, saw Shams, stopped, and sat in the room directly opposite. For some time, they stayed motionless, looking at each other silent and intent. No one knew who Shams was nor why Rumi was sitting there.
>
> Then Shams said, "Maulana, may God's mercy be upon you, what do you say about Bāyazīd*? They say he never ate a melon, because he said he never heard about the Prophet

* Ninth-century Persian mystic about whom Shams was particularly critical.

eating a melon. What do you say about such a man? He was so precise and meticulous in following the Prophet, yet he said, 'Oh God, how great is my status!' and claimed that none was in his cloak but God. In contrast, the Prophet, the one with such grandeur and glory of rank, said, 'I feel worry in my heart sometimes, and seventy times a day I ask God to forgive me.'"

Rumi replied that Bāyazīd had reached a particular station of sainthood and had become stuck there because the "glory and grandeur of that state prevented him from seeing any further." He continued that the Prophet differed markedly in that he had never stopped moving toward perfection and apologized to God for delaying at all in the lower stations. Then Shams and Rumi emerged from their respective chambers and embraced.[76]

The flash of recognition had ignited the fire of profound spiritual love between the two, and it would continue burning for the rest of Rumi's life. Rumi's response to Shams' question proved his readiness for Shams' instruction. As Shams said:

> Maulana perfectly understood the full implications of the problem and where it came from and where it was leading. It made him ecstatic because his spirit was so pure and clean and shone on his face. I realized the sweetness of my question only from his ecstasy. Before then I had been unaware of its sweetness.[77]

The teacher, aged about sixty-two, had found his disciple, who was not yet forty. Rumi was immediately and deeply drawn to Shams. Sultan Valad, Rumi's son and second successor, says that his father "became totally and completely absorbed in the effulgence of Shams al-Din's light. Within the warmth emanating from Shams' attractive words, Rumi saw Shams' unity with the divine. He laid both his heart and head at Shams' feet."[78] Rumi said:

> For lovers, the beauty of the beloved is their teacher.
> His face is their syllabus, lesson, and book.[79]

Sultan Valad says that these feelings were the same for Shams, who had asked God for the company of a soul who could bear his friendship.[80] As Shams said:

> My first condition for coming to be with Maulana was that I did not come as a sheikh. God has not given birth on earth to anyone who is Maulana's sheikh. Such a one could not be human. I am not someone who can be a disciple either. That is not left in me.
>
> Now, because our relationship is only for the sake of friendship and comfort, I should not have need for any hypocrisy. Most of the prophets have not expressed reality. Hypocrisy means to express that which is different from what is in your heart. "He who knows his mind, knows his God." In reality, it is, "... knows Me." He [the Prophet] was too shy to say it, so he said, "... knows his God." However, had he not spoken in this way, his companions would not have been able to bear it. Yet it is a kind of hypocrisy that will take them to heaven. His sincerity will take them to *Haqq*. Whoever was more receptive to his sincerity became closer to the world of *Haqq*. Now I am Maulana's friend, and I am sure he is one of God's saints. The friend of God's saint is God's friend. This is the way it is.[81]

In the *Masnavi*, Rumi captures this reciprocal search and longing:

> The thirsty one asks,
> "Where is the sweet, delightful water?"
> The water likewise asks,
> "Where is the drinker?"[82]

Rumi had no doubt about Shams' identity. He says:

> You are that Light who told Moses
> "I am God, I am God, I am God."[83]

WITH SHAMS – INTOXICATION WITH THE BELOVED

Following their meeting in the market, Shams and Rumi remained in each other's company in near isolation for several months at the home of Salāh al-Din. Salāh, a goldsmith, had also been a disciple of Borhān and would later become Rumi's trusted companion. Shams means "sun" in Arabic, and Rumi immersed himself in the warmth and brightness of Shams' light:

> With you, life and living –
> without you, death and destruction.
> For you are the sun and, without you, we freeze.[84]

After months of seclusion with Shams, during which Shams shared his secrets, beliefs, and his practice of meditation, Rumi completely undid the strictures of his previous life. Shams said:

> In my presence, as he listens to me, he considers himself – I am ashamed to even say it – like a two-year-old child or like a new convert to Islam who knows nothing about it. Such submissiveness![85]

Rumi even abandoned the scholarly dress of the Islamic jurisprudent in favour of the simple style worn by Shams. He exchanged his white turban for a smoky-coloured one and put on a Sufi cloak made from striped Indian cloth. Later, after Shams' final absence, he had his Sufi shirt and cloak sewn with an open front, out of step with the customs of the time. He wore this for the rest of his life.[86] He set fire to his pulpit and stopped teaching and preaching.

What evolved between Shams and Rumi was no ordinary teacher-disciple relationship. Rumi was already spiritually advanced when he met Shams, a worthy companion for the older man. And yet Rumi was clearly learning a new way of being from Shams. As he said:

> When your love enflamed my heart
> all I had was burned to ashes, except your love.
> I put logic and learning and books on the shelf.[87]

Shams was sometimes harsh in his criticism of Rumi even though his love for him was always unreserved. Rumi understood and accepted the rebukes of his teacher with gratitude:

> O my idol, I am like a tent.
> First you put me up, then you pull me down.
> I am like a pen in your hand.
> First you shape my nib, then you break me.[88]

> Should you pour poison in my cup,
> I would drink it joyfully.
> Whether your wine is mature or immature,
> I'd be immature to reject it.
> Should you serve blood in my cup,
> if I did not treat it as a goblet for the elect,
> I would be unworthy.[89]

Shams described himself as a barrel of divine Wine fully concealed from all, which was opened because of Rumi. He said, "The fact is that we [Shams] are his [Rumi's]. Our intention and the light in our eyes are the benefit he will derive." Shams praised Rumi, telling others that Rumi's discourses had "a hundred benefits," not only because of their content but also simply because of the way Rumi spoke.[90]

Furūzānfar tells us that, to test Rumi's faith and obedience, Shams once asked him for a flask of wine. Rumi purchased a bottle of the best and returned through the market to Shams. Alcohol is forbidden in Islam and Rumi was a respected, well-established Islamic lawyer, so this was a brave display of obedience in the face of likely social consequences. Shams expressed his pleasure, saying, "I was testing his faith and patience."[91]

Rumi's son says that, although Rumi had knowledge of God and was in a position to guide people, he had desired the company of advanced souls and found all the advanced souls he needed in Shams. He tells us:

> At a celebration for the opening of a new madrasa, among a large gathering of the most important people of Konya, Rumi was asked, "Where is the highest, most respectful seat?" Shams-e Tabrizi was new in town and was among the crowd that day. Rumi answered, "For the knowledgeable, it is on a platform; for an Āref, it is in his home; for Sufis, it is alongside the platform; and in the religion of lovers, it is next to the Beloved." With these words, he rose and sat by Shams. That day marked the beginning of Shams' fame in Konya.[92]

If Rumi was profoundly ready for Shams, Konya was not. Rumi was no young seeker on the spiritual path; he was a respected legal scholar with followers of his own and well connected among the ruling class and among the community of scholars and lawyers. Why, many wondered, was he abandoning his family duties, his teaching, and his preaching for the company of a suspect wandering dervish who had a sharp tongue and a withering glance? Shams was impolitic and gruff, and his manner was off-putting. Those surrounding Rumi, already alarmed by the intensity of Rumi's love for Shams, began to be resentful of his part in Rumi's radical transformation. Rumi's son, however, understood:

> Suddenly the sun of religion* came to him.
> He was annihilated in the effulgence of his light.
> From beyond the world of love, a song,
> brought without instrument or tambourine,
> described to him the state of the beloved.[93]

After their initial few months in seclusion, Shams became a member of Rumi's household and focused all his energies on helping Rumi break free of his preconceived ideas about God. He was planting these seeds in fertile soil that had been tilled by Rumi's father when he was a child and later by Borhān. To those followers of Rumi who eyed him with suspicion, Shams made the case that his place in Rumi's household was as a member of the family, with Rumi permitting him to be in his young wife's company:

> Don't you wonder about my admittance into this [Rumi's] house and how he has made his wife – upon whom if Gabriel gazes, he is jealous – my confidant?[94]

Although Rumi appreciated the didactic poems of Sanā'i and Farid al-Din 'Attār, he was not particularly attracted to poetry in general. Following Shams' instruction, however, he stopped reading entirely and began to compose poetry himself.

Shams was in the habit of practising *samā*, which was frowned upon by many and even banned by orthodox Muslims. He says:

> In *samā*, God manifests and can be seen more frequently by men of God. They go beyond their own world of existence. *Samā* brings them out of these other worlds and unites them with the sight of God's face.[95]

---

* Shams (sun) al-Din (religion).

In Shams' company, Rumi became transformed from a socially conservative Islamic lawyer into a wild, abandoned dervish who attended *samā*. He became the prince of the Persian Sufi poets, pouring out devotional verse. In the *Masnavi*, Rumi says:

> When free of ego, men clap their hands;
> when they leap out from self, they dance.
> Musicians within them play the drum;
> the sea foams from their zeal.[96]

And so he danced, intoxicated on the divine Wine of love and on his beloved Shams, who had unlocked the creativity of his heart and set it free:

> Your love made me drunk, made me clap my hands.
> Drunk and unaware of myself, what can I do? . . .
> People are saying, "You should not be that way!"
> I wasn't like this – he made me this way![97]
>
> I always had the Koran in my hands,
> now, in love, I have musical instruments.
> I had God's praises in my mouth,
> now I have poetry, couplets, and ballads.[98]

After several periods of seclusion with Shams, Rumi attempted to resume his role as a religious leader in Konya. Yet, when he returned to lecturing, he brought Shams with him. Though a learned man with a wide breadth of knowledge, Shams spoke in enigmas and riddles. He often taught by telling stories and weaving tales to emphasize his points and to make them memorable. He emphasized action, the need to experience the spiritual path and to put in the work in order to reach the beloved. He said:

> Someone takes you as a guest to a garden to eat walnuts. He climbs the tree, starts picking and cracking open walnuts, and invites you to come and pick and shell some walnuts for yourself. Your hands and sleeves turn black in the process.
>
> But another man takes you as a guest to a garden, has you sit in a nice place, and tells his servants to do the work. They pick the walnuts from the tree, shell them, and even take the second skin off. Then, when they serve the clean, fresh walnuts to you, asking you to eat them, you instead say: "What kind of walnuts are these? I never heard the cracking sound and my hands and sleeves did not turn black. I will not eat these. I have never seen such a thing as this before. God knows what these are."[99]

Combined with his rough appearance and manner, Shams' methods and style of teaching appalled Rumi's disciples, who could not understand why their teacher was deferring to someone as unpolished as Shams. Given his complete immersion in Shams and withdrawal from them, it is not surprising that the hostility of Rumi's followers towards Shams increased steadily until it became a simmering wrath. More than once, Shams asked Rumi to keep them in line but Rumi was unable to do so. It may be that, as these were his father's companions and their sons, he was conflicted about his obligations. It also seems possible that Shams wanted him to learn about separation from the physical form of the beloved so that he could focus on the internal beloved. Whatever the case, the rejection and hostility became the reason that, just sixteen months after his arrival, Shams left Konya abruptly and without warning.

THE PAIN OF SEPARATION

Rumi was devastated by Shams' absence and stopped writing. If his followers had hoped for him to resume his old routines now that Shams was gone, they found that Rumi was deeply disconsolate and became even more withdrawn than before. Having been transformed by Shams, he was unable to go back to his previous state, yet he could not progress in his current mode without Shams to guide him. He started a desperate search for his teacher and began sending servants to find him. It took one month for Rumi to find out that Shams was in Damascus. After many letters went undelivered or unanswered, he sent his son Sultan Valad and a large entourage with poetry and gifts to beg Shams to return. In the message from Rumi that Sultan Valad delivered to Shams, Rumi apologized for the behaviour of his disciples and assured Shams that they had repented. He was unable to compose any poetry until he received a letter from Shams. After hearing from Shams, he composed five or six ghazals where he speaks of his desperate state of separation. These letters in verse to Shams are among the earliest of his poetry that we have:

> Oh you, light within my heart, come!
> Goal of all effort and desire, come!
> You know my life is in your hands.
> Do not oppress your worshipper, come![100]
>
> From the moment you went away
> I was stripped of sweetness, turned to wax.
> All night long I burn like a candle,
> scorched with fire, but deprived of honey.
> Separated from your beauty, my body
> lies in ruins and my soul is a night owl.[101]

Shams agreed to return and, upon arriving back in Konya, was greeted with celebration and fanfare. He and Rumi resumed their intense and exclusive relationship with Rumi beginning to understand the effect of their painful separation on his spiritual development:

I sleep and wake in love's afflictions.
My heart turns on the spit of passion's fire.
If you abandoned me to best refine me,
you are wise and I'm, without you, unrefined.

This absence would kill me the moment you left
if each day I did not expect to meet you.
I repent prayerfully, beseechingly
to my lord for my sins and shortcomings.
Tabriz radiates with my lord, faith's Sun –
I weep blood, choke on it for what I've done.[102]

Shams moved back into Rumi's home and, soon after, married Kimiyā, the much younger girl who had been raised in Rumi's household. Rumi, seeing this as an opportunity to cement Shams' place in his family, was overjoyed. Though little is known about their relationship, both Sepahsālār and Aflāki write about the disruptive effect it had within Rumi's family, specifically with his second son, Alā al-Din. Whether resentful of Shams taking his place beside his father or jealous of Shams' marriage to Kimiyā, tension between Rumi's son and his beloved Shams became knife-sharp. Then, only months after their wedding, Kimiyā died suddenly after falling ill after a walk in the garden with other women in the house. After this tragic event, Shams was, once again, confronted by the rising hostility, jealousy, and negativity of Rumi's followers who never seemed to grasp the importance of Shams to Rumi. Sensing that his time in Konya was nearing an end, Shams began to speak of disappearing for good, a final separation that would finish "cooking" Rumi's spiritual development and force him to find the beloved within. Rumi expressed that final stage this way:

The sum of my life is but three words –
I was burnt, I was burnt, I was burnt.[103]

One morning, Rumi went to Shams' quarters and found his beloved teacher and companion gone. Rumi burst into his son's room, shouting, "Bahā al-Din, get up! Again I feel the nostrils of life are devoid of the perfume of his grace."[104] When Shams did not return and could not be found after two days, the void of his absence engulfed Rumi whole. It had been only three years since Shams had arrived, completely disrupting Rumi's life. Now Shams was gone and Rumi was bereft.

AFTER SHAMS: LAMENTATION

The lingering rumour was that Shams was dead. Rumi refused to believe it and could not find a remedy for the pain of separation. Disturbed and deeply distressed, he composed verses that gave voice to his disbelief that his human guide was gone but still showed that he understood the real nature of his Beloved:

> Who says the eternally living has died?
> Who says the sun of hope has died?
> The enemy of the sun goes to the roof,
> closes both eyes, and says, "The sun has died."[105]

On one occasion, a disciple hammered a nail onto the door of what had been Shams' room. Hearing the sound of the hammer, Rumi cried, "Don't they know whose room that is? They are pounding the nail into my heart!"[106]

The news and rumours continued. Rumi took a strange comfort from what he heard. Even though tales were always fabricated and unreal, he would encourage travellers to tell him their stories:

> For a moment, tell the tale of Tabriz,
> for a moment, tell the tale
> of those blood-spilling glances.[107]

He was so enamoured with these tales that, when someone told him that they had seen Shams here or there, he would immediately give the storyteller his turban or his cloak and thank him profusely. One day, he was told that Shams had been seen in Damascus. Rumi expressed his joy and gave the man his turban, his cloak, and his shoes. A friend said to Rumi, "The man is lying; he hasn't seen Shams." Rumi replied, "I gave what I gave because he lied; if it were the truth, I would have given my life."[108]

Understanding that he had been left, Rumi was ravaged by overwhelming pain and grief:

> I am that black night, angry at the moon,
> I am that naked beggar, angry at the king.
> The grace of that Peerless One
> was calling me home,
> but I made an excuse, angry at the path![109]

Yet despite his inner turmoil, Rumi knew that the physical form of his beloved Shams was gone.

FINDING THE BELOVED WITHIN

After many unsuccessful searches, Rumi became restless and held prolonged sessions of *samā*, dancing and whirling day and night, all the while pouring out his devotion in the poems we have come to know as the *Divān-e Shams-e Tabrizi* (*A Collection of Poems of Shams of Tabriz*). Rumi's son Sultan Valad gave us the entire story in a long poem that includes:

> Now say what separation has done to that king:
> dancing in *samā*, day and night;
> whirling like the sky, but on the earth.
> His wail and cry reached heaven.
> All heard his lament, young and old.

To musicians he would give silver and gold
and all he possessed.[110]

In a contemporary Persian book on Rumi's spiritual development and his relationship with Shams, Mohammad Ali Movahed describes Shams' view of the three stages of his disciple's spiritual transformation leading to his final realization. At first, Rumi was still raw, not yet empty of self, trapped in ego, and proud of his own authority over knowledge of the world. In the second stage, his existence was completely drowned in Shams and he is heedless of all others except Shams. Finally, Rumi became a perfect man in the making – a saint who is consciously aware of the presence of God – although not yet fully manifested.[111] At this point, Shams left Konya, hastening a final stage of Rumi's spiritual development. Rumi's ultimate joy of realization came hard on the heels of the most painful experience of his life.

Forty days after Shams' disappearance, Rumi turned over responsibility for all his disciples to Sheikh Salāh al-Din and travelled to Damascus for what would be the last time. He stayed longer than expected. Aflāki tells us that Rumi's disciples were greatly distressed by his absence from Konya. The Sultan ordered a letter to be written and signed by all the great and good of Rum. It was sent to Rumi inviting him to return to the place where his father was buried. Moved by this gesture and always kind, Rumi returned to Konya to continue guiding people on the spiritual journey.

Rumi's son Sultan Valad writes:

He said: Although physically I am away from him,
without body and soul, we are both one light.
Either you see him or you see me.
O seeker, I am he and he is I.
He said: if I am he, what am I searching for?
I am his mirror image; now I will speak.[112]

Later, Rumi composed a long eulogy that is among the translations in this book, *On the Death of Shams, ghazal 2893*. He sums up his glorious relationship with Shams in *Fih-e māfih* with words that reflect his own transformation:

> The lighted lamp kissed the unlit lamp and went away.
> He fulfilled his aim.[113]

Finally, Rumi says:

> Why should I go on searching the world
> when my beloved is within?[114]

Sepahsālār tells this story about Rumi's devotion to the inner beloved:

> One time on an early winter night in his madrasa during prayer, Rumi had prostrated and cried such copious tears that his face and beard were frozen, stuck to the floor. In the morning, his companions had to pour warm water over his face until the ice melted. Such was his outer prayer. Who knows the condition of his inner prayer![115]

Rumi's zealous *samā*, frequent fasting, sleepless nights and endless prayers were done to purify himself enough to attain constant union of his soul with his beloved. As a result, he received the ultimate divine Truth, the awareness of the constant presence of the beloved within himself, the real goal of spiritual teachings. Aflāki recounts how Rumi says he has become the "beloved":

> Because mystics in the past were sometimes accused of breaking the law, and because of that, imprisoned or even killed by the religious class, Rumi's son Bahā shared that on

one occasion, he was thanking God that his father was still intact with the family. Rumi then smiled and alluded to his own position as the beloved, saying, Bahā al-Din, the rank of "Beloved" is different than the rank of "lover." The beloved is a commander who is obeyed at all times, but the lover is the one who bears all troubles.[116]

Similarly, in the following verses Rumi refers to his attainment of union:

> Anything you seek in the world is not outside of you.
> Seek what you want within yourself, for it is you.[117]
>
> There is no one but God in my cloak.
> How long will you search the earth and sky?[118]

AFTER SHAMS: RUMI THE PUBLIC FIGURE

The actual time that Rumi spent with Shams was a very small fraction of his life, and yet it transformed him completely. After Shams left for the second time, Rumi's desire was to immerse himself in meditation and commune with the inner beloved. However, there was still work for him to do in the world, part of which was to instruct others how best to live in the world and how to do the inner work *they* needed in order to reach God.

Rumi was a public figure for much of his life. After the departure of Shams, he lived, wrote, and guided his community for another twenty-five years. He had assumed many roles: student, lawyer, preacher, disciple of Shams and, finally, beloved teacher. His kindness and generosity of spirit had always made him appealing to a broad base of society, regardless of status. He seems to have been indifferent to politics, recognizing that he might be able to influence the powerful but not regarding them as central to his purpose. He did have a relationship with Sultan Ezz al-Din

Kay Kaus II, who probably came to power while Shams was still in Konya. The sultan ruled until 1260 and may have considered himself Rumi's disciple; Rumi certainly wrote to him and provided him with reminders that the world is not to be trusted. He also assured the sultan that loss of temporal power did not mean that God had ceased to look after him. Rumi corresponded with a variety of other powerful figures, almost always, it seems, to provide spiritual advice, although occasionally to seek help for his extended family.

Aflāki also tells us that Mo'īn al-Din Solaimān Parvāneh, a powerful politician who was a sincere devotee of Rumi, threw a great party that included *samā*. The zeal with which Rumi started the *samā* caused a lot of hubbub but Rumi was absorbed and unaware. One among the eminent was talking to Parvāneh, expressing surprise that Rumi's followers were mostly artisans rather than from groups of the knowledgeable and illustrious. He was saying, with some scorn, that whether tailor, carpenter, or grocer, Rumi accepts them all. Suddenly Rumi, still engaged in *samā*, shouted so loudly that everyone was astounded, "O ignorant one, wasn't Mansur a cotton carder, Sheikh Abū Bakr a weaver, and the other one a glass maker? What harm did their profession cause their understanding?" Parvāneh and the other man could only apologize.[119]

Thus, at least as important as his interactions with rulers was Rumi's relationship to the poor, the workers, and people of other religions. Rumi maintained relationships not only with the scholars and rulers but also with ordinary Muslims. Communities within cities in this period tended to cluster by religion: Jews, Zoroastrians, Christians, and Muslims remained largely separate, yet Rumi would engage with all of them. He dealt with the powerful, the lowly, and even children, with humility and with humour. As with all great mystics, Rumi ignored worldly rank, religion, gender, and race. He was interested in disciples who sought God. Indeed, he once pointed out to a ruler who criticised him for his disciples and their bad character that his (Rumi's) role was to reform and remake humans; if they were of good character, Rumi said, he would have followed them, not vice versa. Consistent with this, Rumi focused on those who sought God; there were no other preconditions. It was in this spirit that Rumi regularly gave time and attention to the women among his disciples, without concern for whether such practice violated societal norms or rules. Aflāki relates in the following story:

> ... every Friday, all the wives of the eminent of Konya gathered in the house of the Sultan's special secretary. They would beg his wife to invite Maulana Rumi, because Rumi gave her so much grace and was so attentive to her, calling her "Sheikh of the Ladies." The women would gather and wait for him with focused attention. Meanwhile, their husbands gathered outside the house with the Sultan's secretary, talking and guarding the place, so that common people wouldn't come to know their wives' secret.
>
> When the afternoon prayer finished, Rumi would go to them alone and unannounced. The women would circle around him, pouring roses and rose petals over him while he spoke to them about inner meanings and mysteries. Finally, female musicians would begin to play flutes and tambourines, while Rumi began *samā*. Those women's states would transform into such ecstasy that they would pour their gold and jewellery into Rumi's shoes, hoping he would accept something, but he would not even look at their offerings. Rumi would stay with them until morning and leave after performing the prayer at dawn.[120]

Aflāki also tells us that, in explaining why he folded his sleeves, Rumi said that the entire universe is like a wonderful and grand *khānqah* (a Sufi hostel) whose real teacher is Allah; all the Saints, prophets, and special devotees are like travelling Sufis. He continued, saying that when a Sufi unfamiliar with the *khānqah* enters and does not know which person is the servant, he should look for the one with the folded sleeves and realize that this is the servant from whom he should learn all the other rules and manners. He noted that from then on, the new arrival could stay at the *khānqah*; otherwise, the residents would throw him out. The story concluded with Rumi's clear instruction that it is our destiny to follow the example of the Prophet, who said, "The Master of a tribe is their servant."[121]

Indeed, Rumi was extremely modest. If his followers tried to move someone out of his path, an embarrassed Rumi would leave immediately. He would never let anyone know that he had given them money. He would put small allowances under each seat cover in his madrasa and when the students shook off the dust, they would find his gift. Aflāki also tells us about his humility in this story: in *samā*, Rumi was in a state of ecstasy when, suddenly, a drunk entered the circle and bumped into him. Rumi's disciples shamed and insulted the man. Rumi reprimanded them, saying, "*He* has drunk the wine and *you* are acting badly?" They said, "He is a Christian," and Rumi said, "Then why don't you become a Christian?"[122]

Nonetheless, Rumi's upbringing, worldly study, intelligence, and fluency in communication put him in the uppermost tier of society. At his core, however, were his morality, his understanding of the unity of everything, his surrender to the divine, and the peace and love he had for all. He never responded to the immoral or destructive behaviour of others with a harsh word or a bitter answer; rather, through kindness and example, he would aim to bring about change. Sultan Valad says that Rumi once said to him:

> Bahā al-Din, if you want your enemy to like you and you to like him, say good and decent things about him for forty days; then he will become your friend. In the same way that there is a path from the heart to the tongue, there is a path to the heart *from* the tongue.... The more purity there is in a heart, the more God's radiance will shine in that heart. It is like a

baker's oven: as long as it is hot, it will accept the dough; once it is cold, it will not.[123]

Rumi always encouraged his followers to work and provide for their own needs, telling them that all the past Saints permitted their followers to carry a basket and beg for food to make the disciple humble. In contrast, Rumi said that he had closed the door of asking, following the Prophet's order that each person, with his own effort, should provide a legitimate livelihood for himself.[124]

He himself provided for his family's needs through his teaching and legal opinions and did not accept support from the powerful. He lived with little and whenever there was nothing, he would happily declare, "Today our home is like the Prophet's home."[125]

One day, an Amir sent seventy thousand drachma to Rumi who ordered that it all to be sent to Hosām, one of his companions and his successor. Rumi's son said, "We have nothing left at home . . . whatever is coming, my father sends it to Sheikh Hosām al-Din." Rumi said, "Bahā al-Din, I swear to God three times that if a hundred thousand perfect ascetics face emaciation from hunger, and I have just one loaf of bread, I will also send that to Hosām."

Sepahsālār tells us that Rumi was a man who led an ascetic life: he ate and slept very little, even in old age. After days and nights of *samā*, if his followers wanted to sleep or even rest, they did not allow themselves to do so in his presence. Aware of their anxious state, Rumi would pretend to sleep, sitting with his back to the wall, his head on his knees. His servant would cover him with a large cloak and, when all the disciples fell asleep, he would get up and begin to pray, sometimes again moving and turning. Sepahsālār tells us that Rumi lived without sleep: "In the forty years that I was in his company, I never saw him with any sleeping attire or pillow or lying on his side to sleep. His pining for God's love was a constant moving factor in his body, which had become accustomed to strict, rigorous discipline."[126]

Aflāki gives us a story that illustrates the depth of Rumi's knowledge, both worldly and otherwise:

> Rumi was giving a Friday sermon before a large crowd. Loud approving shouts greeted his masterful use of unusual examples to support his discourse on Koranic verses known as Surats. In his heart, a scholar who was present thought, "It is easy to talk when you know the subject you want to speak about, but if you can talk about a random Surat in this way, then that would be mastery." Rumi turned to him and asked him to recite some Koranic Surat from memory, which he did. Rumi expounded on it so thoroughly and precisely that the lawyer started to shout and kissed the legs of Rumi's pulpit. Everyone was spellbound, enjoying the talk; the discourse lasted into the afternoon. Rumi said, "When you sit in the presence of the special ones of the Divine, watch your heart and sit attentively and with sincerity so that you can partake of their eternal good fortune. They are spies of all hearts."[127]

That sermon was Rumi's last.

AFTER SHAMS: FINDING THE BELOVED IN OTHERS

Rumi neither preached nor accepted any worldly positions after Shams left, but he helped and guided some disciples through his poetry and *samā*, familiarizing the gentle-natured with the subtle truths about being human and occasionally calling rulers and commoners, people of all religions, to the path:

> My heart bleeds in separation from you but
> from that blood, soulful faces have sprung to life.[128]

Salāh al-Din

One of these "soulful faces" belonged to a disciple of Shams named Salāh al-Din Zarkūb-e Ghounavi, the goldsmith with whom Shams and Rumi had stayed in the months after they first met. Although guiding seekers of truth and disciples was the norm among Sufi *murshids,* Rumi now appointed Sheikh Salāh al-Din to undertake this task:

> Salāh* of the heart and faith
> is certainly the image of that Turk.†
> Rub your eyes and look:
> the face of the heart, the face of the heart.[129]

His love for Salāh grew into an unbreakable spiritual bond. Salāh al-Din was from Konya, and his friendship with Rumi began while both were students of Borhān. Both became disciples of Shams but, by this time, Rumi was a God-realized Sufi sheikh. Salāh al-Din became his friend, his companion, and his mirror. It is as though Rumi were telling the world and his recalcitrant followers that, although they may have driven away the physical form of his beloved Shams, he could show them exactly how it would have been if Shams were still with them. Indeed, Sultan Valad says:

> That Shams-e Din of whom we always spoke
> has come back to us! Why do we slumber?
> Changed into new clothes, he has returned
> to flaunt and strut and show his beauty.[130]

Salāh al-Din became the focus of Rumi's poetry and looked after Rumi's followers. He also became the public preacher and

---

* *Salāh,* in Persian, means "advantage or virtue."

† Shams.

teacher in Rumi's place and, as Franklin Lewis speculates, may also have become the conduit for the workers and artisans who felt pulled towards a spiritual life.

Salāh was a simple uneducated man who did not even pronounce certain words correctly, so others considered him ignorant and common. The people of Konya would see him in the bazaar working as a goldsmith every day and, like those whom Rumi had earlier rebuked over their inability to comprehend that spiritual and worldly rank are not related, failed to understand how he was worthy of being a sheikh and capable of leading seekers to the Truth. Despite his favour of Salāh al-Din, some of Rumi's followers created problems as they had with Shams, provoking Sultan Valad to make a direct comparison. He tells us that the enmity reached a point where some of them even plotted to kill Salāh. When he heard about it, Salāh laughed and said, "Without God's order, not even a leaf moves; if he gives the command, one must obey. Even though they wish to kill me, I will speak nothing but good of them." Then he said, "They are jealous because Maulana has chosen me. He sees himself, not me – how could he not choose himself?"[131]

When the news reached Rumi, he banished these followers. Yet again, the followers repented, and Rumi and Salāh forgave them. His compassion and forgiveness were such that they extended even to this dangerous group whose contrition appeared only after they had been completely excluded from Rumi's presence. No longer threatened, Salāh continued in his appointed role and even became a spiritual guide for Rumi's family. Rumi had taught Salāh's daughter, Fateme Khatūn, to read and write. She married Rumi's son around 1250, and thus Salāh became Sultan Valad's father-in-law as well.

Rumi openly praised Salāh and humbled himself before him to such a degree that Salāh felt embarrassed. In this ghazal, Rumi expresses his love for him without hesitation:

> On the day of resurrection,
> no one will come to the rescue,

> but Salāh al-Din, Salāh al-Din, and that's that.
> If you know the secret of his secret,
> stay quiet – do not reveal it.[132]

Once, when Rumi was passing through the goldsmiths' bazaar, the sound of hammering on gold made Rumi start *samā*. Seeing that, Salāh ordered his employees to continue hammering the gold for Rumi's pleasure; Rumi recited this verse:

> In that goldsmith's shop,
> a treasure appeared.
> What form and what meaning –
> what goodness, what goodness![133]

Salāh al-Din died in 1258. His last wish was to have his body carried with joy and songs of *samā*, rather than the usual expressions of grief: his soul was free and returning to its home. Rumi, without his turban in a visible acknowledgement of loss, and among a crowd of others, shouted enthusiastically. Turning and dancing in *samā*, they went to Rumi's father's tomb and, with joy and love, buried Salāh.

From the elegy Rumi composed for Salāh:

> O, in separation from you,
> heaven and earth weep.
> My heart is sitting in blood –
> my mind and soul weep.[134]

In the *Divān*, there are about seventy ghazals that end with the name of Salāh al-Din.[135] Salāh was a quiet and peaceful man and after spending ten years in his company, the fire ignited in Rumi by Shams had become calmed and contained, if burning just as brightly. Rumi had found the Beloved within and without – in

Salāh and, soon, in another companion: Hosām al-Din, who is also known as Chelebi.

Hosām al-Din

The family of Hosām al-Din Hassan ebne Mohammad ebne Hassan was from Urmia, Iran. They moved to Konya, where Hosām was born in 1225. In the introduction to the *Masnavi*, Rumi calls him, "the key to the treasuries of God's throne and trustee of the treasures on earth, Bāyazīd and Junayd of our time."

Hosām was not yet an adolescent when his father died. Although many members of his extended family offered to instruct him, he went to Rumi and became his disciple. He gave away most of his possessions and freed his servants – encouraging them to learn skills to support themselves – leaving himself with only the bare necessities of life. When Salāh al-Din was still living, Hosām followed him. When Salāh died, Rumi turned to Hosām and made him the leader of his followers.

Rumi's love for Hosām was such that whenever he was asked to speak, Hosām was required to be present; thus, those interested would first make sure that Hosām was invited. Their companionship gave us the *Masnavi*, probably the greatest and most magnificent of Sufi writings. The story is that Hosām had observed that Rumi's followers, even though they had Rumi's *Divān*, would read poetry from great poet-mystics such as Sanā'i and Attār. So Hosām asked Rumi to write a book in the style of Sanā'i's *Walled Garden of Truth* or Attār's *Conference of the Birds*. At that very moment, Rumi pulled from a fold of his turban the first eighteen stanzas of the *Masnavi* and gave them to Hosām, saying, "I will compose; you will transcribe."[136]

Thus it was that Rumi dictated the *Masnavi* to Hosām al-Din; Hosām wrote down and sang back the extemporized verse for Rumi's approval. He is described as Rumi's muse in each of the six books of the *Masnavi*. Through years of turmoil that were not only political but also, due to the loss of his wife, personal for Hosām, he and Rumi worked tirelessly on its composition and its recording. Some nights, as is evident from the *Masnavi* itself, this would go on until morning.

Sepahsālār tells us this story about the way Rumi cherished Hosām:

> Often, Rumi would stay at Hosām's home. One winter night, he arrived late; the door was closed, everyone was asleep, and heavy snow was falling. In order not to disturb anyone, Rumi neither returned home nor knocked at Hosām's door. He stood there with the snow falling on his head. In the morning, when the servant opened the door, he saw Rumi standing covered in snow. Hosām came out and fell at Rumi's feet, crying and apologizing repeatedly, while Rumi consoled him and kissed his forehead.[137]

Hosām's wife died after the first volume was completed, which delayed the *Masnavi* for two years. Then, from the year 1263, they started on the second volume and worked together until the end of Rumi's life. Their companionship lasted fifteen years, during which Rumi delegated all external relations and management to Hosām. Before Rumi died, he appointed Hosām as his successor.[138]

UNION WITH THE BELOVED

Toward the end of 1273, Rumi became ill and developed a fever that did not resolve in spite of his physicians' efforts. When the news reached the public, people began to visit. Hosām recounts:

> One day Sheikh Sadr al-Din, along with some of the great dervishes, went to visit Rumi who was sick with a high fever. His physicians had lost hope of healing him. Seeing Maulana in that state, Sadr al-Din was very sad and said, 'May God give you health. You are the soul of the people of the world,

thus deserving of total recovery.' Rumi said, 'May God give you health now applies to you! In reality, only a garment of poetry is left between lover [Rumi] and beloved. Wouldn't you prefer that garment be removed to let the light unite with the light?' Rumi then composed these lines:

Even if your dress is fashioned
from the finest silk of Shūshtar,
an amorous embrace while wearing no dress
is sweeter and better by far.

I have become free from my body and free of thought.
I am strolling in the utmost state of union.

Sheikh Sadr al-Din and his companion left, weeping, and all Rumi's disciples started to cry. Then Rumi began composing the ghazal:

'How do you know what a king
I have as a companion within?'[139]

Composing poetry throughout the weeks and months of his illness, Rumi's verses became suffused with the happiness and release of death, which would end the separation from God at last. He referred to his death as his "wedding night" for the union it would bring with the Beloved and composed the following poem on his death bed, addressed to his weeping son, Bahā:

The only cure for my pain is dying
so how may I ask him to cure my longing?
Last night I dreamed
I saw an old man in the alley of love.
He waved to me with his hand,
as if to say, "Come to me."[140]

On 17 December 1273, as the sun was setting, Rumi left the world at the age of sixty-six. The whole town attended his funeral, including Jews and Christians. When Muslims asked them why they had attended, they answered, "If he was like Muhammad for Muslims, he was like Moses and Jesus for us; and if he was your leader, he was also ours, for he was aware of our hearts and souls."[141] Sultan Valad writes:

> The eye of mankind wept bitterly that day.
> Lightning struck and burned away the souls.
> Quakes rolled through the earth that moment.
> In the heavens rose a wail of mourning . . .[142]

But Rumi says:

> The day you see my coffin being carried,
> do not imagine I am in pain, missing this world.
> Don't cry for me and don't say, "Alas, alas!"
> for "alas" is when one falls into the demon's trap.
> When you see my corpse,
> don't say, "Farewell, farewell"
> for that is the time of my meeting and union.
> When you leave me in the grave,
> don't say, "Goodbye, goodbye"
> for the grave is a veil over the peace of paradise.
> When you see the setting, see the rising also –
> how could setting be a barrier for the sun and moon?
> What seed went to earth and failed to grow –
> why, then, imagine that about a human seed?
> It appears to you that I go beneath the dust
> but the seven skies will be beneath my feet.[143]

Rumi was buried in his family mausoleum near his father's tomb and mourning lasted forty days. The great line of spiritual power that passed from Shams-e Tabrizi to Rumi continued through Hosām al-Din and then to Rumi's son. The Mevlevi order, which takes its origin from Rumi's teachings, is still active and flourishing.

⟶⟵

For the last twenty-five years of his life, Rumi wrote continually on spiritual knowledge and spiritual practice, leaving us five great works: *Maktūbāt, Majāles-e Sab'eh, Fih-e māfih, Divān-e Shams-e Tabrizi,* and *Masnavi.* The poems that we know as the *Divān-e Shams-e Tabrizi* are profound declarations of love. They are an aching cry from the heart – the voice of longing that separation from the Beloved produces. Within these lines, we find love and pain, wisdom, and the ecstatic joy of union. And, to this day, we find a constant reminder of the path home to God.

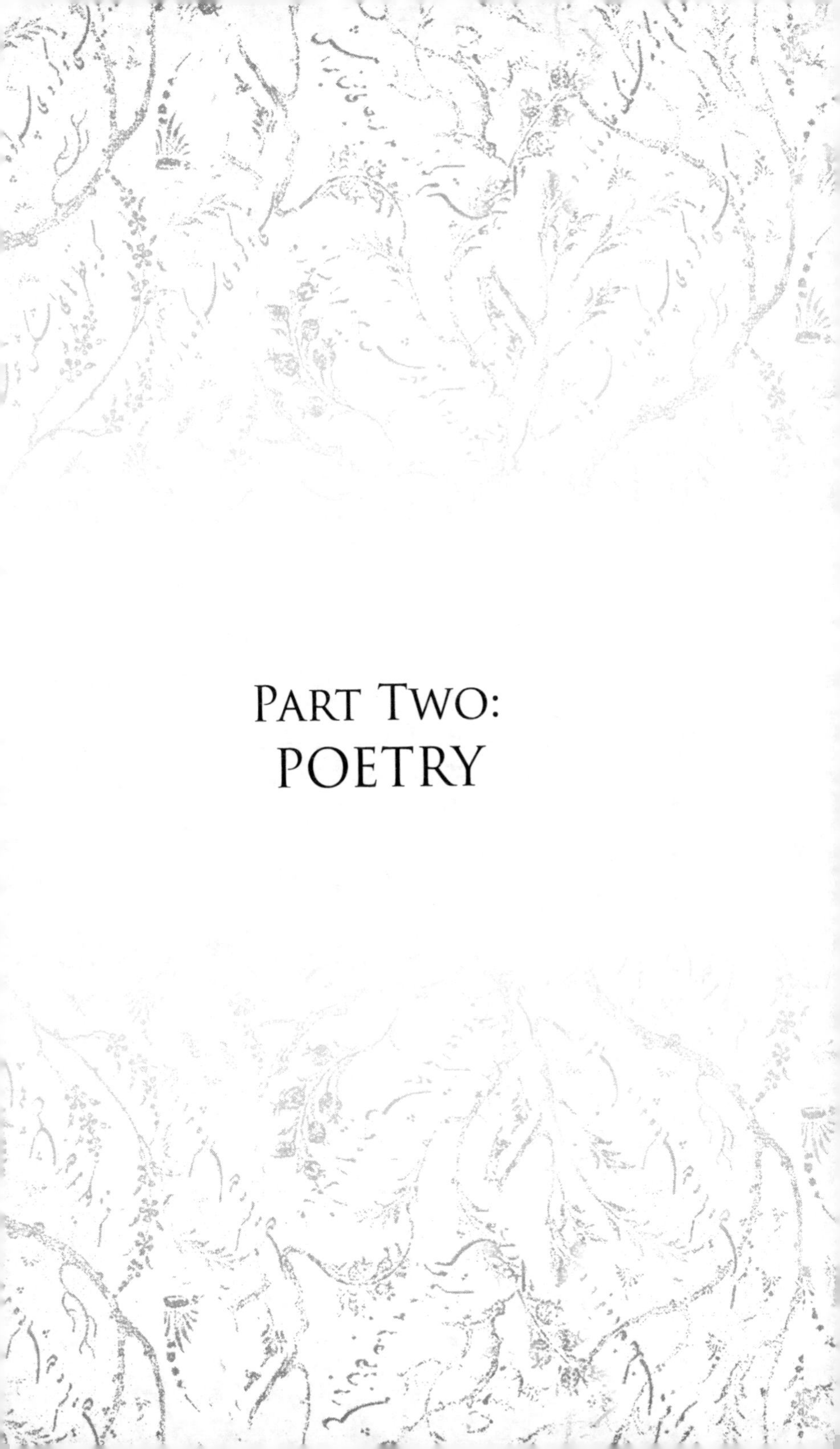

Part Two: POETRY

Our Only Hope

The joyful rhythm of this first poem suggests that it may have been composed when Rumi was in samā. We see the contrast between our absorption in sensual pleasures and the beloved's power and purity.

O you,
sudden rebirth and endless grace,
you set the thicket of our thoughts ablaze.

Today you come laughing
as key to the prison –
as God's sweet forgiveness
you come to the suffering.

You are our only hope, gatekeeper for the sun.
You are seeker and sought, beginning and end.

You fill our hearts, you adorn our thoughts.
You make a wish and you also grant it.

O you,
matchless exhilaration,
you are the joy of knowledge and action.
All else is excuse and deception,
for this is the illness, that the potion.

With vision twisted by deceit
we are nasty to the innocent.
At times, we are drunk on doe-eyed beauties,
at others, on soup and bread.

See my drunkenness, leave wisdom.
See my sweets, end your story.
So much drama –
just for bread and vegetables!

You devise a plan of a hundred colours
to wage an illusory war
between black and white.

You pull the soul's ear in secret
while blaming others.
"Lord, set me free!" pleads the soul,
"I swear all is a game, O Lord."

Shh!
I'm in a rush to take refuge
with the Conqueror.
Put down the paper and break the pen –
Saqi has come with the invitation!

ghazal 1

Into the Whirlpool

Rumi teaches us about the world and the path to escape.

O lovers, O lovers,
today you and I have fallen
into the whirlpool.
Now let's see who can swim!

If a flood fills the world
and each wave is as big as a camel,
birds of the water won't worry,
but birds of the air will.

Our faces aglow with gratitude,
we're as at home in the sea and waves
as the sea and typhoons
are life-giving to fish.

O sheikh, hand me a towel.
O water, tumble me around.
O Moses, come and split the sea
with your staff.

This wind* cooks a different passion
in every head.
Let passion for that *Saqi* be mine –
let all the rest be yours.

*Desire.

Yesterday, on the road,
that *Saqi* stole the lovers' hats.
Today, he is giving us wine
so he can take away our cloaks!

O you, envy of Venus and the moon,
yet with us, hidden like fairies,
you are pulling gently, joyfully,
but won't you at least say to where?

Wherever you go, you are with me.
O you, my eyes and the light of my eyes,
pull me to either drunkenness
or annihilation, as you wish.

The world is like Mount Sinai,
we are seekers like Moses.
Every moment, the Lord manifests
and splits the mountain.

One part grows verdant,
another fragrant with narcissus.
One part becomes pearl,
another ruby and amber.

If you want to see Him,
look at His Mountain.
O Mountain, what Wine did you drink
to make us drunk on Your echo?

O Gardener, O Gardener,
why entangle us?
We took Your grapes,
but You took all we had!

ghazal 14

Your Head is the Ladder

Rumi talks of God, then has a conversation with Shams in which he is told of the soul's inner journey using the Koranic story of the night Gabriel took Muhammad to "the farthest mosque" and "saw something of God."[*]

Today I saw the friend,
the splendour of all You do.
Like the soul of Mustafā,[†]
He rose into the sky.

The sun felt ashamed of his face
and the sky was tattered
like a heart in love.
By his radiance,
the light of water and clay
was brighter than fire.

I said, "Show me the ladder
to climb to the sky."
He said, "Your head is the ladder –
just step on it.
Put your foot on your head,
step beyond the stars.
Once you crush desire,
come, step into the air!
There, across the sky,
a hundred paths will appear.
Every dawn you will fly
like a prayer to the sky."

ghazal 19

---

[*] K 17:1 and 18:53.
[†] Muhammad; a reference to K 17:1.

Fly Back

We are not grazing animals – we are falcons.

The sky calls out
to souls every moment,
"For God's sake, come up!
How long will you linger
on earth like dregs?"

The sluggish lie on the bottom like dregs –
when they are purified,
they will rise to the top of the barrel.

Stop stirring the mud
so the water becomes clarified.
Then your dregs will be purified
and your pain will be healed.

The soul is like a flame,
but its smoke can overwhelm its light.
If the smoke billows unchecked,
no light will shine in the house.

Smother the smoke and
benefit from the light of your flame.
Then both this house and the other
will be brightened.

If you look into murky water,
you see no moon, no sky.
The sun and the moon are hidden
when the air darkens.

The north wind is blowing
and clears the air –
the breeze of dawn polishes it.

Breathing polishes the heart,
blowing sorrow away.
If the breath stops for a moment,
the mind will die.

Alien in this world,
the soul longs for the city of No-Place.
Why should the animal-like mind
remain grazing here for so long?

O pure and noble soul,
how long will you travel?
You are the king's falcon – fly back
to the sound of his call.

ghazal 26

AN INVITATION

Listen to the sounds of the bell and the flute.

O lovers, O lovers,
now is the time for meeting and union.
A call came from the sky,
"O you, with glowing moon-like faces,
here is your invitation!"

O drunken lovers, joy is coming,
gracefully strolling.
We have clung to her chain,
she has clung to our skirt.

O demon of sorrow, go!
The fiery wine is coming.
O life that ponders death, go!
O eternal *Saqi,* come!

Oh, the seven skies are drunk on You.
We're like a marble in Your hand.
Oh, a hundred thousand praises
for Your existence, the cause of ours!

O sweet-breathed minstrel,
keep ringing your bell every moment.
O bliss, saddle your horse.
O breeze of dawn, breathe on our souls.

O sweet story-telling Sound of the flute,
we taste the sugar in your Sound.
Morning and evening, the fragrance of faith
reaches us from your Sound.

Play once again, play those melodies.
O lovely-faced sun,
be coy with all the beauties.

Stay quiet, don't rend the veil,
drink the ample cup of the quiet ones.
Be concealed, be concealed,
imbibe the patience of God.

ghazal 34

My Mind

No pleasure in the world matches divine love.

Because only love for your face
can bring contentment to my mind,
abandoning this desire
is profane to my mind.

Because your love
brought my mind back to life,
how can I wage a war with it?
Your murderous, amorous glance
is the *hajj* and *jihad* for my mind.

Because the curl of your hair
is home and hearth for my mind,
only the form of a shadow
remains of my mind.

Love kindled a fire
that put the Water of Life to shame.
You ask me, "For whom?"
I answer, "For my mind."

Eighteen thousand worlds
of pleasures and wishes were offered.
Except for love of your face,
no other desire remains in my mind.

Hell is for the faithless,
paradise for the faithful,
love is for lovers.
And annihilation?
Just a reward for my mind!

O essence of true faith,
core of contentment's secret,
O lord of my soul, Shams-e Din,
you purified my mind.

I exchanged my soul's sweet fragrance
for the dust of thousands of stones from Tabriz.
It forms the collyrium that lights my mind.

ghazal 52

Tell Your Own Story

The first four verses speak of the hidden secret. The next four advise us to escape to the inner regions. The last eight remind us that every disciple's relationship with the teacher is unique.

O heart, don't stay even one breath away
from the realm of good fortune.
One moment, drink the wine of the soul –
the next, chew on sugar.

Inside is divine wisdom –
outside, an armful of roses.
One moment the inspiring command, 'Say'* –
the next, the honour of 'We granted.'†

Knowing 'the most hidden secret'‡
and its trials and celebrations
brings visions of the divine
and joy without regret.

The beauty adorning every face
is a drop of that Ocean,
but how can the parched be quenched
with just one drop?

O heart, there is a way out
of this cramped prison into the open air,
but your limbs have gone to sleep
and you think you have no legs.

---

*Many Koranic *āyats* start with the word *qol* (Say!), God's command to Muhammad.

† K 108:1; "We granted" refers to God's gifts to humanity.

‡ K 20:7; the inner path.

What nourishing portions hide
behind the daily bread you seek!
My dear, these breads far surpass
the baker's craft!

With eyes closed, you ask,
"Where has the bright day gone?"
Then the sun hits your eyes, saying,
"Here I am! Open the door!"

They pull you this way, they pull you that.
O most pure, don't descend to the dregs.
Let go! Reach the top!

Any thought hidden in the quiet of your chest
signals its colour from your heart to your face.

O dear one, the inner state of every tree
shows on its leaves and branches,
shaped by the seed through which it drinks.

Drinking from an apple seed, apple leaves grow.
Drinking from a date seed, a crown of dates grows.

Just as a doctor diagnoses
by seeing a patient's colour,
a sage knows your religion*
from the colour of your face
and the state of your eyes.

---

* In Islam, religion (*dīn*) prescribes how one should act in every sphere of life.

By your colour,
he sees the state of your faith,
your loves and hates,
but he conceals it
to save you from disgrace.

Though he sees your letter,
he will not read it aloud,
but he certainly knows, O letter bearer,
what form you will deliver tomorrow.

If he speaks about what he sees,
he will hide it in allusion and mystery.
If you are seeking ardently,
you will understand his signs and subtlety.

But if you are not seeking ardently,
I will say this to you clearly,
"You will only know the story of others
and repeat that wherever you go."

ghazal 54

THE SEA OF FORGIVENESS

Rumi describes Shams and the inner beloved using images from the Koran and Sufi lore. He then describes how we are lured by the "gentle signs" of the creation and fall into the well of vanity, from which the beloved offers rescue.

Your body is that precious night
bringing us good fortune.
Your soul is that full moon
parting the curtain of darkness.

You are God's almanac
holding so many predictions.
You are the sea of forgiveness
washing away our sins.

You are the 'protected slate'*
teaching hidden mysteries.
You are a merciful treasure
giving robes of honour to others.

Strangely,
You are the 'much-frequented house'†
being encircled by angels.
Amazingly,
You are the 'scroll unrolled'‡
flowing with nectar to all.

---

* K 85:22.
† K 52:4.
‡ K 52:3.

You are beyond why and how,
an unparalleled soul.
All ponderings about you
turn upside down.

Because your light shone
upon the creation
from beyond why and how,
our affection was given – in error –
to Your gentle signs.

You are a wondrous Joseph –
a hundred wells reflect
your moon-like beauty
by which every Jacob has fallen
into the trap of the human well.*

You make a rope from your hair,
pull us from the well,
carry us to mercy's embrace, and
free us from bewilderment.

Quiet!
Words and examples don't work here.
Pass beyond bewilderment and
you will comprehend His attributes.

ghazal 55

---

* See the glossary for the stories of Joseph and Jacob.

Ask the Hoopoe

Prepare for the king who understands what we need and opens the inner door. In Farid al-Din 'Attār's Conference of the Birds, *the hoopoe refers to the sheikh.*

The king is coming!
The king is coming!
Decorate your doorway
and cut your hands
over that Canaanite's* beauty.

When my soul's very life is coming,
it's not fitting to talk about life,
for what use is life,
except as a sacrifice at his feet?

In the absence of love
I was led astray,
but suddenly love appeared.
Though I had been a mountain,
I became hay for the horse of the king.

Whether he is Turk or Tājik,†
this slave is close to him
like the soul is close to the body –
but the body cannot know.

---

*Joseph.
†All people.

Hey friends!
Good fortune has arrived!
It's time to offer your body.
Solomon has taken the throne
to rid us of Satan.

Why be so lethargic?
Get up! Why delay?
If you don't know, ask the hoopoe
the way to Solomon's palace.

There, offer your supplication.
State your needs and secrets.
Solomon knows the language
of each and every bird.

O devotee, talk is like the wind
scattering the heart –
but by His command,
the scattered will be gathered
together again.

ghazal 58

Yearning

This poem can be read as Rumi longing for the physical presence of Shams or as the lover longing for the presence of the inner beloved.

My ear awaits your message.
My soul longs, with life itself, for your greeting.

In my heart, the blood of yearning is boiling,
awaiting the scent of your bubbling wine cup.
Oh, with your enchanting charm and sweetness,
your snare needs no bait.
Kings have offered their crowns and belts
to adorn the cloaks of your lowliest servants.

When this love began, I thought I knew
how you would end it.
Chain me to the leg of your camel.
How could I ever covet a seat on its back?
Whoever drinks the milk of your grace
will surely die if weaned.

Swear upon the words of the Unseen Revealer
that you will whisper your message in my ear.
Swear upon the house that bestows good fortune
that you will show me your roof from afar.
If a head gains by bowing before you,
what loss is there from the grace you bestow on all?

Shams-e Tabriz, this enamoured one
has tied your name to his heart.

ghazal 248

Day and Night

Rumi is being played like an instrument: restless, joyful, intoxicated, distressed, and tearful.

Restlessly longing for you – day and night,
I lay my head at your feet – day and night.

I make the day and night crazy, like me.
How could I let them be just
day and night?

Lovers are asked to give their hearts and lives.
I offer my heart and life –
day and night.

Until I know what is happening in my head,
not for one moment can I rest –
day and night.

From the moment your love became the musician,
sometimes I became a harp, sometimes a *tār*[*] –
day and night.

You pluck my strings
and my wailing reaches the sky –
day and night.

You became man's *Saqi* for forty mornings,
shaping him with your hands.[†] I still feel drunk –
day and night.

[*] A Persian stringed instrument.

[†] A hadith, 'He moulded Adam with his hands for forty days,' refers to creating the human form.

O you who hold the lovers' reins in your hand,
I am also in this caravan –
day and night.

Drunk and unaware, I carry your load like a camel.
I am under this load –
day and night.

Unless you break my fast with your sweets,
I am fasting until resurrection –
day and night.

When my fast is broken at the table of your grace,
my life will be Eid* –
day and night.

O you, life of my day and night,
I am waiting, I am waiting –
day and night.

I need not wait a year to celebrate Eid.
With your moon, I have Eid –
day and night.

Since the night you promised the day of union,
I've been counting the days and nights –
day and night.

The field of my love is so parched with thirst
that teardrops rain from the cloud of my eyes –
day and night.

ghazal 302

---

* A celebration to end the month of fasting.

I Will Not Leave You on the Road

The beloved is talking to the soul that has reincarnated from body to body (many "stations") and is now being taken home. This last journey requires patience and persistence, time and pain, grace and love – all gifts from the beloved.

I have come to pull you to me by the ear –
to seat you in my heart and soul,
to make you lose your heart and self.

I, sweet spring, have come to you,
O rosebush, to draw you joyfully to my side,
to scatter your petals.

I have come to this house to beautify you,
to take you, like lover's prayers,
above and beyond the sky.

I have come
because you stole a kiss from an idol.
Give it back happily, good man –
or I will take it.

A rose? No. You are essential
because you recite the command: 'Say.'
Even if no one else knows you, I do,
because you are me.

You are my life and my soul –
you recite the prayer[*] for me.
Transform yourself into prayer
so I can recite you in my heart.

O my prey, you are mine,
though you have escaped the trap.
Go back into the snare –
or I will lead you there.

The lion said to me,
"Go away! You are such a rare deer.
Why do you run so fast after me?
I could tear you apart."

But no, you are a lion cub
hidden in the body of a deer.
I will take you, once and for all,
out of your hiding place.

You are a shield of courage –
accept the blow and proceed.
Hear nothing but the bowstring
and I will bend you like a bow.

[*] Referring to the *fatiha*, the first *sura* of the Koran, which is recited several times in each of the five daily prayers and also when someone dies.

Thousands of stations exist
between dust and the human form.
I have led you from town to town –
I will not leave you on the road.*

Say nothing, don't froth,
leave the lid on the pot.
Keep boiling patiently,
for I am cooking you thoroughly.

You are my polo ball,
struck by the polo stick
of my command.
Though I have made you run,
I am running after you.

ghazal 322

* Rumi also uses "from town to town" in ghazal 1509, the cycle of birth and rebirth.

With You and Without You

The opening line of the first five verses refers to our ego. When we give up our desires, we gain everything.

The moment you are with you,
the friend is like a thorn to you.
The moment you are without you,
what's the use of the friend?

The moment you are with you,
you fall prey to a mosquito.
The moment you are without you,
an elephant is your prey.

The moment you are with you,
you are bound to a cloud of sorrow.
The moment you are without you,
the moon comes to you.

The moment you are with you,
the friend stays away.
The moment you are without you,
the friend's Wine comes to you.

The moment you are with you,
you are as cheerless as autumn.
The moment you are without you,
winter looks like spring to you.

The moment you seek rest,
restlessness comes to you.
Seek restlessness
so rest comes to you.

Your indigestion is because
you seek digestion.
The moment you ignore digestion,
even poison is wholesome to you.

Your failure to obtain your wish
is because you seek your wish.
Otherwise, all wishes would be granted
as a gift to you.

Fall in love with the friend's cruelty,
not his kindness,
so the coquettish idol
will fall madly in love with you.

When Shams-e Din, King of the East,
comes from Tabriz,
I swear to God you will feel ashamed
to gaze at the moon and stars.

ghazal 323

We Enter that Stream

The madman vanishes with the king into the Stream of living water.

I am mad
because of that king
who has no desire
for drum and flag –
and, as a madman,
I can't be held responsible.

You'll see me from afar
as someone passing by.
I'm just a fleeting thought,
non-existent.

Become non-existent,
for that is the source of life –
and not just a life of grief and sorrow.

I without me
and you without you
will enter the Stream,
for nothing exists
in this dry land
but tyranny and abuse.

Drowned in this Stream
but alive we will be,
for this Water of Life holds nothing
but grace and generosity.

ghazal 331

The House of Love

The human body – the house of the soul – is special. It conceals, then reveals, the path home. Those who just sit at the entry waste the most precious opportunity.

This house –
where the sound of the bell
is constantly ringing –
what kind of house is it?
Ask the owner.

If it is the house of Kabah,
then what is this face of an idol?
If it is a Magus monastery,*
then what is this light of God?

A Treasure beyond the two worlds
lives in this house.
The house and its tenant
are just an excuse.

Don't touch the house, it's under a spell.
Don't tell the tenant, he's drunk every night.

Musk and amber are its dust and straw.
Verse and melody are its roof and door.

Whoever finds a way to enter this house
will become the king of Earth
and the Solomon† of time.

---

*Zoroastrian temple.
† A powerful ruler.

O good man, for once,
look down from the roof.
Auspicious signs are visible
on your good face.

I swear that, other than seeing
your beautiful face within,
all else is just a spell and a tale.

The garden is perplexed by your beauty –
what a leaf and what a blossom!
The birds are captured by your beauty –
what a bait and what a snare!

You are the House of Love,
without shore or limit.
You are the Lord of time,
lovely as Venus and the Moon.

Like a mirror, the soul
has taken your image into its heart.
Like a comb, the heart
has run through the tips of your hair.

O Soul, come to me!
My life stands front and centre,
like the women who cut their hands
in Joseph's presence.

The whole house is drunk.
No one knows who might come in –
important or not.

Enter the house right now!
Don't sit at the threshold –
it's inauspicious!
Darkness will overcome those
who sit outside.

Those drunk on God are one,
even if they number a thousand.
Those drunk on passion are of many kinds.

Enter the thicket of Lions*
and don't think about getting hurt.
Even thinking of fear is a form of weakness.

Inside, you won't be hurt
for all is mercy and love.
But behind the door,
your imagination is like a latch.

Stay quiet, O heart,
don't set the thicket on fire.
Hold your tongue – that flame of fire.

ghazal 332

---

* The company of past masters.

THE INNER WOLF

Control the mind that devours us from within.

Our fear comes entirely from inside,
though our attention is constantly outside.

We caress our outside
as if it's a rare beauty like Joseph,
but inside is a wolf seeking to drink our blood.

Our heart would burst if we could see
how ugly that wolf is inside!

No matter how ugly, one attack will kill it
but we have made ourselves inferior to it.

The wolf, now superior, should be made inferior
to make the inferior superior again.*

Without the Lord's grace and generosity
how could the wolf ever become motionless?

Before the world, or humans,
or pure, gentle, flowing souls existed –
even then – Shams had command and kingship,
so don't think this just happened.

I don't have to say being king was his destiny,
but it is true – and a hundred times more!

* Rumi uses the letters *alif* ا and *noon* ن to present this concept.

My Lord, Shams al-Din of Tabriz,
is beyond the seven blue wheels.*

Destiny is tamed under his thighs,
even though it is restive and swift.

When universal wisdom
got a whiff of his nature,
day and night, it became mad with desire.

It had seen great ambition and effort from others
but all were inferior to his.

In which direction can I seek his company?
His dwelling place is beyond direction.

Difficulties unsolved by past great lions
are mere tales and plays for him.

Know that all I've described
are just branches of his true state.
I have not yet spoken of his mysteries.

O Tabriz, your dust is my collyrium,
a dust filled with many wondrous qualities.

ghazal 335

*Inner skies.

Modes and Melodies of Love

To impress upon Rumi the depth needed in order to cultivate love for God, Shams would behave differently in ways that Rumi compares to different musical modes (scales). In Persian, the same word (pardeh) means both musical style and veil, or curtain, so Rumi is making a subtle play on words.

O tell me, dear friend, what mode of behaviour is this?
You have changed again – what mode is this?

Strange! O beautiful-coloured Turk,* what colour is this?
Odd! O amorous eyes, what mode is this?

You are acting coy and it's killing me again.
What bait and snare are these – what mode is this?

You tore our veil – what scale is this?
Remove the veil – what mode is this?

I am that ancient love who, yet again, fell in love.
What mode is this?

Giving your life for that song is allowed.
What a life-giving song! What mode is this?

O Muslims! Behold this fervour!
It is beyond compare. What mode is this?

The wine, the love, the colour – all three are false.
One concealed† and three false – what mode is this?

ghazal 345

* Refers to Shams.
† Shams.

Thief of Hearts

Beginning with a line from another poet (Sanā'ī Marvazi), Rumi sings of the beauty and imperishability of the inner Beloved.

You are perfectly skilled at stealing hearts.
I am ill and in pain, having lost my heart.

Other than with your lovely face, a love affair
is forbidden, forbidden, forbidden.

Everyone and everything perishes,
but celebration of your oneness
is forever, forever, forever.

When I rub my eyes, except for you,
who else is there? Who else? Who else?

For the sake of concealing you
the world is a veil, a veil, a veil.

With every breath, from the tongue of love
comes a greeting, a greeting, a greeting.

From every particle, without a word
comes a message, a message, a message.

Before your throne, our joys and sorrows
are slaves, slaves, slaves.

Though the camel of sorrow[*] is like a wolf,
it is the leader, the leader, the leader.

After that, the milk-laden camel of joy[†]
marks the end, the end, the end.

Not the kind of milk from which the baby
of the soul is weaned, weaned, weaned.

But the milk – the stream of paradise –
that flows steadily, steadily, steadily.[‡]

In the nose of these two camels
is your rein, your rein, your rein.

I keep quiet because, over my mouth,
divine jealousy[§] is a bridle, a bridle, a bridle.

ghazal 356

---

[*] The caravan starts with the pain of separation.
[†] It ends with union.
[‡] Rumi uses a word that means orderly, constrained, and eternal.
[§] A shield that protects the lovers' spiritual interests.

A Hidden Pearl

Parvāneh was a rich and powerful Prime Minister and a devotee of Rumi. Here he learns about the difference between spiritual and worldly wealth.

Because that mine of generosity is what we hunt,
ten thousand gifts come to us with every breath.

He extends a ladder of silver and gold for us
when we seek to reach the beloved's roof.

In the world, calamity is a hidden pearl:
to others, a snake; to us, a treasure.

Don't show off your treasury of silver
for we have immeasurable silver and gold.

If this were Parvāneh's false accusation,
the king accuses me two hundred times more.

ghazal 357

WONDERING

Shams has gone and Rumi longs for his physical presence – and for union with the inner Beloved.

That sugar-pouring beauty – how is he?
That lamp for eyes and sight – how is he?

I wonder about that tale-bearing amorous glance – how is it?
I wonder about that swindling ringlet – how is it?

I wonder about that famed one in the market of goodness.
I wonder about that splendour of the rose garden –
how is he?

My heart sits in mourning for love.
I wonder about that beloved within my heart –
how is he?

By his grace, that friend called me friend.
I wonder about that friend without this friend –
how is he?

He tends to devotees openly.
I wonder when he shares mysteries with a devotee –
how is he?

When I first saw him, he gave me life.
Seeing his generosity,
at giving I know how he is.

If he repeated that generosity, with that repetition
I would certainly know how he is.

I wonder about his silky, wavy hair around his satin face –
how is it?

Ask the physician of lovers about his lovesick narcissus –
how is it?

I wonder about that musk of *Tatār* – how is it?
I wonder about that ringlet of *Bulghār* – how is it?

I wonder about that precisely drawn circle,
that breaker of a hundred compasses – how is it?

I am mournful, held captive by high-pitched wailing.
I wonder if he will ever ask about me, "How is he?"

When my heart stole a glimpse, he stole my heart.
I wonder about that thief who captured this thief –
how is he?

O friend, because I am your friend of the cave,*
peek inside the cave and see how it is
so that, when I see you, I can give up my life
to show others how to look at you – how it is.

My talk has no end, but at least
I have shown the shape of such a talk – how it is.

ghazal 358

* "Friend of the cave" refers to Abū Bakr, the Prophet Muhammad's disciple and friend, with whom Muhammad hid in a cave while running away from enemies in Mecca; also means the inner cave, the focus of meditation.

To Pull You Back

To push us in the right direction, God sends us both the malady and its remedy.

Shall I give you words, sweet as candy,
or tell you tales about the Fountain of Life?

If you put your cheek on my cheek,
I'll tell you why the king checkmated you.

He set your crop on fire
to give you some of his own.[*]

He made you fresh as a field of greens
to buy you back from trifling things.

Rejoice, because he will rescue you,
like Abraham[†] in the fire of love.

When the scroll of your account
was torn apart by love,
your wisdom beheld the night of power[‡]
and a hundred celebrations.

I will swear only on your gentle shadow.[§]
I will not swear on Your essence.

---

[*] When ego leaves, God fills the heart.

[†] K 21:52–71; Abraham was thrown into the fire for burning idols in the temple and was saved by God.

[‡] The night Muhammad received the Koran.

[§] In Persian culture, this is an act of extreme courtesy.

If souls are drowned in your qualities,
how can they ever reach Your essence?

He made us like a stream, humble and flowing,
to wash us of our sins.

To pull us back to that place of No-direction,
He sent us troubles from all directions.

You said, "I'll keep quiet," but you did not.
Love is laughing at your resolve.

ghazal 368

The Most Precious Monastery

Rumi teaches us about love, which takes us to the top of the mountain.

Someone asked, "What is the way?"
I said, "To leave your desires."

O you, in love with the King,
your way lies in seeking contentment
for that hero.

If you want to gratify the wishes of the friend,
seeking to gratify your own wishes is forbidden.

The soul becomes wholly transformed
into love for the beloved,
for this love is the most precious monastery.*

Love for Him is nothing less than the summit.
Our task is complete on that mountaintop.

Love is that cave where the beloved lives.
His radiant beauty gives stability to the soul.

Whatever makes you pure is good.
I will not specify which or what.

Be quiet and attentive to the *pīr* of love,
your leader in both worlds.

ghazal 374

* Monastery means isolation, celibacy, renunciation, separation from the world.

A Game of Chess

As the flood of the self merges into the ocean of love, the ego vanishes, the mind becomes still, and only the beloved remains.

O you,
checkmated by the king of love,
don't be angry or vengeful.
Enter the garden of annihilation
and behold the many paradises
in your eternal soul.

When you go just a little beyond yourself,
past these skies, you will see
the king of truth and meaning –
and his banners and pavilions
made of ancient light.

Don't try to perform a miracle
when you see them,
for miracles are only signs.

The flood is visible until it reaches the sea.
When it drowns, where is it? Gone!

Shams-e Tabriz, you have checkmated* us.
Now we send you a hundred greetings
and a hundred desires to serve.

ghazal 378

* Rumi uses the Persian word *māt* (meaning "from us to you") in the last line, a pun on *shah-māt* (meaning "checkmate") used in the first line.

Killing Lovers

Describing the death of ego at the hand of the beloved, Rumi uses "sideless side" for the omnipresent beloved.

O you, who have plundered my heart,
may my soul and a thousand others
be your prey!

What is your job except killing lovers?
What is your task except killing people?

Kill! May your arm stay strong!
Oh, may the life of the whole world
be an offering to you!

I have seen many killed, yet still alive,
by the amorous gaze
of your half-open, drunken eyes.

I have seen many restless, yet motionless,
in the fire of your tireless love.

Not even one of the dead will stay buried
if you bother to visit their tombs.

With every breath, my soul kisses
the dust of Your footsteps,
drawn by the fragrance of Your sideless side.

ghazal 379

Beware

Although that good man has sharp ears,
he is obstinate and his goods are expensive.

Feeling confident with his false smile,
I thought I was safe because he was quiet!

Beware!
He is cunning – a sea seething under straw.

Intelligence is a key wherever you go.
But with him, it's a lock. What can you do?

He looks at your face and smiles.
Don't feel confident – it's a disguise.

Any heart that falls into his grasp
always moans like a harp.*

In spite of all this, he is nectar
and souls circle around him like bees.

He is a lion. In awe of him,
sorrow sleeps like a mouse in its tomb.

Shams-e Tabriz, the day has dawned.
Why is the world absorbed in last night's tales?

ghazal 380

* A pun; *chang* means both "grasping hand" and "harp."

Useless

Rumi speaks of receptivity to love using the four states of matter as metaphors: water, earth, air, and fire.

When your heart is not with me,
companionship is useless.
If you are like that,
though you sit with me,
it is useless.

When your mouth is shut
while your heart burns with thirst,
if you enter a stream
and just look at the water,
it is useless.

When a body is devoid of soul,
it is devoid of pleasure.
If your huge platter is empty of food,
it is useless.

When the earth is filled to the sky
with the sweetness of musk and ambergris,
if you cannot smell,
it is useless.

When you flee from fire,
you stay raw and sour, like dough.
If you sit with countless
heart ravishers and beloveds,
it is useless.

ghazal 389

Become the Beloved

Eliminate concepts and desires – and walk the path of lovers.

Love is not found
in knowledge and learning,
in books or on pages.
Whatever people talk about
is not the way of lovers.

Know that the branches of love
are in eternity, its roots in infinity.
This tree is not supported by
the earth, the sky, or a trunk.

Dismiss wisdom and limit your desire,
for neither intellect nor character
is worthy of this glory.

As long as you have desire,
know that desire is your idol.
Once you become the beloved,
you become existence –
you have no more desire.

A man in the sea clings constantly
to a plank of hope and fear.
When the man and the plank are destroyed
they can do nothing but submerge.

Shams-e Tabrizi,
you are the sea and the pearl.
You are the very secret of the Creator.

ghazal 395

A Joyful Celebration

This poem is particularly beautiful in the Persian language. It contains many references to the Koran and Sufi metaphors. Each stanza ends with the word "drunk" (mast) – not on alcohol, which is forbidden, but drunk on the Wine of God.

Look!
Because 'God is their *Saqi*'[*]
all the *Abrār*[†] are drunk.
On His eternal beauty,
the seven, five, and four[‡] are drunk.

See this resurrection
manifesting from the Unseen.
On the Wine of God,
the barrel, jug, and heavenly pool
are drunk.

The bodies of lovers
are like shadows on the earth,
but in the heaven of love
'beneath which the rivers flow,'[§]
their pure souls are drunk.

As God's beauty manifests
more and more, then see:
like Moses, bit by bit,
both worlds are drunk.

---

[*] K 76:21.
[†] K 76:5; believers.
[‡] Seven inner skies, five senses, four elements.
[§] K 2:25 and 65:11.

Because of the drunkard's request
and God's answer, "No, you can't see Me,"[*]
every hair of their mediator,
Ahmad-i Mukhtār,[†] is drunk.

Muhammad is the head
and we are the turban wrapped around it.
On the Wine from the other side,
the head and the turban are drunk.

O Joseph of Egypt,
lower your gaze to look at Egypt;[‡]
see the town in an uproar
and the whole marketplace drunk.

O brother, you will be dazzled
if I tell you of this wonder:
God's throne, the earth, and the skies
are all acting drunk!

Shams-e Tabriz
threw a joyful celebration in my heart.
On the wine of love,
the whole place[§] is drunk.

ghazal 398

---

[*] K 7:143; God told Moses that he would not be able to see Him unless the mountain remained standing; it crumbled and Moses fainted.
[†] Prophet Muhammad.
[‡] Joseph denotes the soul; Egypt, the creation or the human body.
[§] Literally, "this door and wall [of the body]".

Sword of Truth

We hear Rumi longing for oneness with the beloved, but the beauty of the physical form can be so captivating that it veils the inner beloved.

O captivator of hearts,
isn't now the time for joy?
O quarry of sugar, the time
to scatter sugar has come at last.

You are the Water of Life
and we are seeds beneath the ground.
Merge with us through your grace –
the time has come.

If I transform like a seed,
I will become a date palm.
From being nothing,
everything becomes something.

O sword of truth, from now on
don't be so sharp with me.
The raging fire is extinguished
by your grace.

I offered up my life before his love
and love said, "Is that all?"
"After all," I said, "my life has become
like this because it has nothing."

Because my outer eyes
veil the eye of my heart,
Shams-e Tabrizi has become a veil
over Shams-e Tabrizi!

ghazal 399

This Brilliant Light

Questions for those who are searching for God.

How long will you keep asking
for a remedy, for a cure?
Who makes you seek a remedy –
who is that?

How long will you be sad
over freeing your soul from sorrow?
You still don't even want to know
what your soul is.

If you follow the scent
of the bread you've been given,
the scent tells you
what that bread is.

If you've fallen in love,
your love is reason enough.
If you're not in love,
why do you seek a reason?

For God's sake,
don't you have the wisdom to see
that if there's no king,
what is this royal court?*

* God's creation.

If that divine Beauty
did not exist within,
then what is this brilliant Lamp
in the hands of your soul?

From a distance
your heart pounds with fear.
How can you know about the brave
and their hearts in that fight?

The fire of saints' eyes
burns unseen veils,
but you're sitting behind the veil
pondering why to believe the unseen.

If Shams-e Tabriz
is not residing in my eyes,
what is this spring of nectar I taste
at the base of every tooth?

ghazal 406

One Essence

Aflāki writes that Rumi said the entire world is contained in one person and recited the hadith, 'O God, guide my people for they do not know.' Rumi further explained that "my people" meant parts of him and that he would not be whole if those without faith were not also a part of him. Rumi then recited this ghazal.[144]

The search of lovers is not their own.
No seeker exists in the world but Him.

The essence of this world
and the other is one.
In truth, there is no heathen,
no religion, no faith.

O you, with your Jesus breath,*
don't talk of separation.
I am a slave of one
who doesn't think of distance.

If you ask, "Should I walk backward?"
No, don't.
And if you ask, "Forward?"
No, the way is not forward.

Open your hand
and grab your own skirt.†
Nothing but this wound
will heal this wound.

---

* Possessing the ability to breathe life into the inanimate or, metaphorically, for breathing spiritual life into those who are dead to their true nature.
† Seek help from yourself.

All the good and bad
are part of a dervish.
Anyone who is not like this
is not a dervish.

For one who has lost his place,
his heart becomes his place.
And like a heart,
he has no place in the world.

One whose heart is caressed
by Shams al-Din's grace
feels no pain
from the sting of his might.

He beats the drum of kingship
in the domain of *faqr*,
but he is not poor –
his treasure is understanding.

ghazal 425

FINALLY

Filled with joy, and celebrating his liberation, Rumi extols the beloved who has come to set him free.

You took abode in my heart and soul – finally
and made them both crazy – finally.

You came to set this world on fire
and did not give up until you did – finally.

Oh, the world has been ruined by your love.
Now you plan to come to this ruin – finally.

O heart, I was trying to keep you busy
but you remembered that fairy tale – finally.

Leaving yourself behind,
you took love to the inner sanctum
and made wisdom a stranger – finally.

O messenger of God,*
like the crying column of Hannānah,†
you made my column of patience cry – finally.

Grace that overcomes troubles
is a candle to the world.
You made the candle into a moth – finally.

---

* Shams.

† A column in Muhammad's mosque in Medina on which he would lean while giving discourses; legend has it that when he left Medina, the column cried in separation.

One of my heads is towards you,
the other faces this direction.
You made me like a two-headed comb – finally.

I was a lowly seed under the soil.
You made the seed into a precious pearl – finally.

You made a garden
into a meadow of flowers from a seed.
You made dust into a home – finally.

O, you Majnūn-like heart,
even worse than Majnūn,
you acted with courage and manliness – finally.

The bowl of the head is filled
and emptied by you.
You brought the bowl into balance – finally.

Through knowledge,
you made rebellious souls
fall in love with the beloved – finally.

Shams-e Tabrizi,
you made every particle
wise and luminous – finally.

ghazal 427

Perseverance

With echoes of an Islamic court of law, here is a list of requirements for lovers – it begins and ends with perseverance.

He asked, "Who is at the door?"
I said, "Your lowliest slave."
He asked, "What do you want?"
I said, "O moon, to pay my respects."

He asked, "How long will you persevere?"
I said, "Until you let me in."
He asked, "How long will you eagerly wait?"
I said, "Till resurrection day."

I claimed, "I am in love!"
I swore many times,
"My courage and authority
were lost in love."

He said, "The judge needs a witness
when there is a claim."
I said, "My tears are the witness,
my sallow face the sign."

He said, "Your witness is unlawful
and your tears* impure."
I said, "By the glory of your justice,
they are lawful and pure."

---

*Literally, "wet." Ritual prayer requires having clean and dry face, hands, and feet; therefore, tears represent ritual impurity.

He asked, "Who was your companion?"
   I said, "Thoughts of you, O King."
He asked, "Who called you here?"
   I said, "The fragrance of your soul."

He asked, "What is your intention?"
   I said, "Friendship and loyalty."
He asked, "What do you want from me?"
   I said, "The grace you bestow on all."

He asked, "What place is best?"
   I said, "The palace of the Emperor."
He asked, "What did you see there?"
   I said, "Limitless generosity."

He asked, "Why is it deserted?"
   I said, "Fear of a robber."
He asked, "Who is that robber?"
   I said, "A critical mind."

He asked, "Where is safety?"
   I said, "In devotion and moderation."
He asked, "What is moderation?"
   I said, "The way to peace and safety."

He asked, "Where is the hardship?"
   I said, "In the alley of your love."
He asked, "How are you doing in there?"
   I said, "I persevere."

Silence! If I tell you about all his subtle points,
   you will break out of yourself.
You will lose your roof and door!

ghazal 436

Sun of Beauty

This poem was composed after Shams left Konya. Every one of these desires is just the unending desire for the beloved.

Show me your face,
for that rose garden and meadow are my desire.
Open your lips,
for that abundant sugar is my desire.

O sun of beauty,
come out from behind the cloud for a moment,
for that glowing, radiant face is my desire.

From the sky
I heard your falcon drum calling me again.
I have returned –
to alight on the Sultan's forearm is my desire.

You said coyly, "Go away, don't bother me."
The way you say, "Don't bother me" is my desire.

The way you push me away and say,
"Go away, the king is not at home" –
that coy playfulness and the gatekeeper's harshness
are my desire.

Attractive people have mere scraps of metal
in their hands.
That mother lode – that mine of sweet beauty –
is my desire.

Bread and water are in flux on the wheel of life.
I am a fish – a whale – and the sea of Oman
is my desire.

Like Jacob, I ceaselessly sigh in sorrow.
The pleasure of seeing Joseph of Canaan
is my desire.

By God, without you the city is a prison to me.
To wander mountains and deserts is my desire.

Downhearted over my weak-willed fellow travellers,
that Lion of God[*] and Rostam the Champion[†]
are my desire.

My soul is weary of Pharoah[‡] and his tyranny.
That light on Moses' face is my desire.

I grow weary when people cry and complain.
The tumult and uproar of drunkards is my desire.

I can speak better than a nightingale sings
yet, because of public envy, my mouth is sealed –
only weeping and wailing is my desire.

---

[*] Ali, companion, cousin, and son-in-law of Muhammad.
[†] A legendary hero in the *Shahnameh* who won every battle, but unintentionally killed his son while fighting.
[‡] The mind.

Yesterday, the sheikh searched the city with a lamp,
saying, "I'm tired of these wild animals and demons.
A human being is my desire."*

They said, "We have looked, but none can be found."
He said, "The one who can't be found is my desire."

Although I am poor, I will not accept
even one small carnelian.
A mine of free, rare carnelians is my desire.

He is hidden from our eyes,
but all we see has come from him.
That concealed yet visible skill is my desire.

My state has gone beyond desire and greed.
From mere space and time
that Essence of all is my desire.

When I heard a story of faith
my ears became drunk.
Where is the share for my eyes?
The face of faith is my desire.

In one hand a cup of wine,
in the other the beloved's curly hair –
dancing openly like this in the marketplace
is my desire.

---

*Diogenes, the Greek philosopher, wandered the city in daylight with a lantern because he needed more light to locate a human being.

That rebec[*] says, "All this waiting is killing me.
Osman's[†] embrace and his pluck on my strings
is my desire."

I am also the rebec of love and my love is like a rebec.
The grace of the Merciful One's strumming
is my desire.

O graceful Musician,
keep playing while I compose the ghazal this way,
for this way is my desire.

O Shams, honour of Tabriz,
show your face from the east!
I am the hoopoe and Solomon's presence
is my desire.[‡]

ghazal 441

---

[*] Stringed instrument.
[†] Osman was one of Rumi's two rebec players.
[‡] Solomon would send the hoopoe with messages to the Queen of Sheba.

In the Stream of the Friend

Rumi tells us that all we see is the friend – yet we don't recognize him.

It is the duty of lovers
to search for the friend.
Like an unstoppable torrent
without regard for their lives,
they rush headfirst into
the stream of the friend!

He is the seeker and we his shadows.
All our talk and conversation
are words of the friend.

Sometimes we flow happily like water
in the stream of the friend.
Sometimes we are confined like water
in the pitcher of the friend.

Sometimes, as we boil like carrots in a pot,
he stirs us with a spatula of thought.
That is the nature of the friend.

He stealthily puts his mouth to our ear
to fill our souls with the fragrance of the friend.

Because he is the Soul of our soul,
we cannot escape him.
In the world, I have not seen one soul
who is an enemy of the friend.

His coyness will melt you
and make you weak as a strand of hair,
but in exchange for both worlds
you would not give up even one hair
from the friend.

Sitting with the friend we keep asking,
"O friend, where is the friend?"
Drunken with pride we ask, "Where? Where?"
even though we are in the lane of the friend.

A weak nature creates bad images
and indecent thoughts.
These are not the way of the friend.

Stay quiet so he will describe his attributes.
Your empty words and noise
cannot be compared
with words and noise from the friend!

ghazal 442

When the Vessel Shatters

Aflāki tells us that Malik Shams al-Din, the ruler of Shirāz, sent a letter to Sheikh Sa'di, an eloquent poet of the time. He said, "Send me a ghazal that includes inner meanings as nourishment for my soul. It doesn't matter who composed it." In return, Sheikh Sa'di sent him this ghazal, newly composed by Rumi.

In the accompanying letter, Sa'di informed the Malik that an auspicious king had appeared in Rum and that nothing better than this poem had ever been composed or ever would be. When he read the poem, the Malik wept and greatly praised it, then ordered a large assembly to gather, and they all performed samā *with it.*

The Malik sent this ghazal to his Sheikh who praised the poem and the poet and then turned to all who were present and said, "It is incumbent on all of you to go and visit this king. I myself am very old now or else I would undertake the trip." Then he turned to his son and said, "I hope your eyes will see that pure sign and will convey our greetings to him." After the Sheikh left the world, his son travelled to Konya to meet Rumi and delivered his father's message.[145]

With every breath,
the song of love
resounds from left and right.
We're going to the sky.
Who wants to come and see the sights?

We have been to that sky
and befriended the angels.
Let's all go again, for that is our town.

We are higher than the heavens,
greater than the angels.
Why not pass beyond them?
Our home is the Divine.

How can this earthly realm
compare with pure Essence?
Where have you landed? Pack up!
What is this place?

Fortune is on our side
and our task is to give up life.
Our caravan leader, Mustafā,[*]
is the pride of the world.

In the light of his face,
the moon could not survive
and so it split apart.[†]
The moon, that lowly beggar,
met with such a fate!

The sweet fragrance of this breeze
comes from the curl of his locks.
The radiance of these thoughts
comes from that face like 'morning light.'[‡]

Look into my heart
and see the moon split
with every breath.
Isn't that why your gaze
is drawn to that sight?

---

[*] The Prophet Muhammad.

[†] Refers to Muhammad's night journey (*mi'rāj*) during which he ascended to the inner skies and split the moon. It describes an internal spiritual experience and a state that Rumi knows with every breath, as he explains two verses later.

[‡] K 93:1.

Humankind, like waterfowl,
is born from an ocean of souls.
Rising from that sea,
how could a bird make this place home?

We are all in that sea –
all of us here are in it.
If not, why does wave after wave
come from the sea of our hearts?

When the wave of *Alast* surged,*
it formed the vessel of the body.
When the vessel shatters again,
it will be the time of meeting and union.

ghazal 463

* K 7:172; literally, "am I not [your Lord]." Refers to the covenant with God.

AWARENESS

An ode to Shams.

With him –
awareness of faith and faithlessness is heathenism.
One who is aware of him shuns the entire world.

Ah – how unfortunate are those aware of all but him,
for his face is like the sun
and his ringlets are scented with amber.
Ah – what a Moses!
If someone beholds him for a moment,
he will shun others as if they were Sāmery.*

His moon has as many buyers as there are stars.
He is desired by as many Mount Sinais
as there are pebbles.

He has blindfolded everyone's eyes.
It is confirmed that his eyes practise sorcery.
He is alchemy and, by the heat of that,
the goldsmith of his love is gilding my face!

O son, like Abraham, put your feet in the fire
for, by His grace, that fire is a garden of water lilies.
The rose garden of his face is the soul's grazing place.
Ah – how the soul is nourished by that rose garden!

In Tabriz, Shams-e Din, that honour of the soul,
found the Pearl of wisdom to see the sea as insignificant.

ghazal 468

---

* K 20:85–98; he made the golden calf that was worshipped in Moses' absence.

Into His Arms

A heart that is filled with the beloved is at peace with whatever he gives.

O sorrow, I won't let you in
even if you're thin as a hair!
My inner state is brimful of sugar,
there is nothing for you here.

Sorrow dwells only in a heart
empty of passion for him.
It enters only where that crafty idol is not.

Even if you become gold,
O sorrow, or pure sugar,
I'll keep my mouth closed –
I will have none of you.

When the heart feels tight,
it is missing his sugar.
If the heart wants to travel,
it is simply into his arms.

Although you are not without sorrow,
reject it and accept him!
If you can't yet see him,
be happy with his fragrance.

The eternal moon is his face
and ghazal and stanza his fragrance.
His fragrance is for those who do not yet see.

ghazal 469

THE VEIL OF POETRY

On the beauty of Shams.

I swear on your gentle, half-open,
drunken, radiant eyes,
and on each curl of your dishevelled ringlets...

I swear on the immeasurable sweetness
and jars of sugar
arranged in your sugar-pouring ruby lips...

I swear on that attractive amber –
that magnet within your ruby lips
by which the sun, moon, and all particles
are drawn to you...

I swear on those heavenly red roses and buds,
snares for the nightingale of wisdom
in your rose garden...

I swear on your freshness and charm
and the radiant, life-nourishing beauty
that opened your mouth
like a laughing pomegranate...

I swear on your divine beauty,
the focal point of all hearts,
before which my soul prostrates
breath after breath in joy...

That you are a Joseph with so many miracles,
but your beautiful face is sufficient proof.

Not only Joseph,
but many Josephs are your captives!
The great and glorious God
would never give you to them.*

If there were space in your garden,
from each and every plant and leaf
a narcissus would bloom to see you.

The king who knows all secrets
would never give you
to those who are cold,
for the fire of your love burns
even the lives of the zealous!

Your face is veiled
in brilliant beams of light.
Like the sun,
you are drowned in divine light.

By your Sun's light,
benevolent with every breath,
you cause a thousand faces
to appear to those with pure hearts.

---

* K 12:19–22; betrayed and abandoned by his brothers, Joseph was sold as a captive to the Egyptians.

If an impure heart wants to hold you within,
it is pulling you to prison in stubborn stupidity.

The wise cannot deceive you
with tricks of wisdom
nor can the honour of kingship bind you.

When your grandeur
cannot be contained in both worlds,
how can Abū Hurairah
assume to have you in his bag?

With every ghazal
where I praise you
through the veil of poetry,
my heart praises you
a thousand times more
behind that veil.

What is my heart, who am I,
and what is this praise?
It is your fragrance that makes my soul
like a flower garden.

Come, O Shams-e Tabrizi,
honoured on all horizons,
you are a rare moon
with incomparable form!

ghazal 486

Flying Free

Attachments bind us to the world and prevent us from seeing the truth.

When you die, you perceive the world of the soul.
When you return to life, you know how to live.

Whoever dies and comes back again like Idris*
teaches about heavenly realms
and knows of the unseen.

Come, tell us by which path you left the world
and by which hidden way you came back again.

It's the path by which all souls,
town after town, fly at night
and why cages are empty of birds at night.

When a bird's feet are tied, it cannot fly very far.
Endlessly circling, it cannot reach the sky
and remains without faith.

If its ties are cut by dying, it flies up and away.
It will see the truth and the secret of everything.

Be silent! Wings are found in the world of silence.
Don't bang the drum of speech for talk is an empty drum.

ghazal 493

* K 19:56–7; a prophet described as exalted to a high inner state, Idris was also known as Enoch in the book of Genesis, father of Methuselah and great-grandfather of Noah.

God is Enough

The difference between Sharia law and the rules for true lovers of God.

Love is nothing but treasure and grace,
nothing but guidance and expansion of the heart.

Abū Hanifa did not teach love.
Shāfi'i gives no account of it.*

The knowledge of 'permitted' and 'forbidden'
goes only as far as death,
but a lover's knowledge is limitless.

Lovers are drowned in sugar water,
yet Egypt† does not complain about a sugar shortage.

How can a drunken soul not feel thankful
for Wine without measure or limit?

If you see anyone sour or full of sorrow,
he is not a lover –
he doesn't come from love's domain!

If every bud were not from a different garden,
then jealousy and envy would not be contagious.

On this path of love,
he who is unaware of how it all began is a novice.

* Founders of two of the four schools of Islamic law.
† Egypt was a major source of sugar.

Destroy your self's existence – annihilate yourself!
No crime is worse than existence of your self.

Don't be a shepherd – be a follower.
Leading is nothing but a veil of wary watchfulness.

To God's devotee,
it is enough that 'God is enough,'*
yet he has neither the knowledge
nor the capacity to grasp it.

He says, "This only hints at Truth and it is difficult,"
but that is clear – that is not an allusion.

When a blind man's foot hit a pitcher,
he said, "The servant has been careless.

Why would a pitcher be in my way?
The path has not been cleared of pottery.

Take the pottery off the path.
Maybe the servant is unaware."

They said, "O blind man,
there is no pitcher on the path,
but you have no knowledge of the way.

---

* K 4:45.

You left the path and hit the pitcher.
You deviated from the path."

O good man,
your intoxication with your religious path
has caused confusion.
There is no *āyat*[*] on how to begin or end.

You are the sign seeking a sign.
There is no better sign
than someone seeking a sign.

It is clear you have no path
because on the path of effort
no one who strives remains without reward.

Because 'evil the size of an atom'[†] is measurable,
an atom of sin is not without consequence.

And 'an atom of goodness is not without reward.'[‡]
Open your eyes if you are not blind.

Every patch of greenery indicates water.
What does not benefit from water?

Stop! This Water has many signs.
The thirsty have no need of guidance.

ghazal 499

[*] Verse of the Koran; it also means a "sign."
[†] K 99:8.
[‡] K 99:7.

The Dance of a Rose

God plays many roles in His creation.

Who is not a slave to Your will?
Who is not drunk on Your beautiful face?

Where is one whose sorrow
is not from separation from You
or whose joy is not from being close to You?

Where is one stingy hand
not caused by Your withholding
or generosity not caused by Your giving?

Where are the ruby lips
that are not from Your mine?
Where is a proud person
who is not a beggar at Your door?

All Your qualities are hidden in every soul.
Not one vein can open or close
without Your command.

Both worlds are like two open hands –
You are the spirit of all.
What can a hand give
that is not from Your generosity?

In this garden of existence,
whose eyes have ever seen
the dance of a rose
that is not from desire for You?

The ignorant moan because of people's cruelty,
but people are like walking sticks in Your hand.

All of these canes are moved by You.
Each one is either Your weapon of pain
or Your crutch of remedy.

Whose stick does the teacher use to punish?
Who is not tied to Your decree?

Like dogs, they bite at Your stick –
they don't understand their punishment.

The physical troubles and harm that people have
are quelled by praising or praying to You.

If you break His stick, does He lack another?
Breaking two or three sticks won't bring you freedom.

Jonah ran away from his sorrows
and lived inside a whale.
Where did he go that did not belong to You?

Stop!
Be cautious – don't get into trouble like Jonah.
Fighting destiny is not in your power.

ghazal 507

Drunkenly

Mercy is what we receive through the grace of God, not what we have earned by our actions. In Persian, there is a touch of melancholy in this poem.

Like a red rose, You pass from hand to hand.
You are like wine, making people drunk – drunk.

When Your forearm won God's bow,
from the world Your arrow[*] leapt out – leapt out.

Your jealousy said, "Go, there is no way out!"
Your mercy said, "Come, yes there is – there is!"

Your grace is an ocean and I am its fish.
Your jealousy fashioned me a fishhook – a fishhook.

Because Your healing balm seeks the injured,
I won't suffer if your fishhook wounds me – wounds me.

O You, who are closer to me than my own breath,
I don't speak near you except softly – softly.

Although there were a hundred wolves
and just one Joseph,
by God's mercy,[†] he escaped – escaped.

Stroll through our town drunkenly
for, by order of our king,
both thief and guard are bound – bound.

ghazal 511

---

[*] The actions of God in the world.
[†] Literally, "by the breath of the Jacob of munificence."

For Hosām

Rumi sings the praises of his chosen successor, Hosām. He is speaking of those intoxicated on the inner Wine and on the beauty of the beloved when he ends each verse with the repeated chorus of "drunkards are saluting you."

Making their souls your servants,
qalandars are saluting you.
Their drunkenness is from your cup –
drunkards are saluting you.

I became
more exposed in love and
more knavish than my peers,
more mirthful among the heart-stealers –
drunkards are saluting you.

Behold the spiritual tumult.
Behold the torrential typhoon.
Behold the divine sun –
drunkards are saluting you.

Can anyone cast a spell on me?
Can anyone ask me to repent?
Can anyone walk without feet like me?
Drunkards are saluting you.

O desire of the desire,
remove that veil quickly!
I know no one but Him –
drunkards are saluting you.

Come, O cloud of the sweet rain.
Come, O drunkenness of the friends.
Come, O king of the swindlers –
drunkards are saluting you.

Be perplexed and be free of pain,
destroy the self and be full of treasure.
Weigh the wealth of eternity –
drunkards are saluting you.

A town is upside down because of you:
aware, yet unaware of you.
You make the heart a beholder
of the inner vision –
drunkards are saluting you.

Tell that prince with the face
as beautiful as the moon,
tell that hypnotic eye,
tell that sweet-natured king,
"Drunkards are saluting you."

Tell that prince of the uproar,
tell that passion and that fervour,
tell that evergreen cypress,
"Drunkards are saluting you."

Where one is not aware of himself,
there is only one drunkard.
No path or faith exists there –
drunkards are saluting you.

Tell that soul without cause,
tell that trap for Majnūn,
tell that hidden pearl,
"Drunkards are saluting you."

Tell that trap for Adam,
tell that soul of the universe,
tell that friend and companion,
"Drunkards are saluting you."

Tell that blue sea,
tell those all-seeing eyes,
tell that Mount Sinai,
"Drunkards are saluting you."

Tell that one who burns my repentance,
tell that tailor of my cloak,
tell that light of my day,
"Drunkards are saluting you."

Tell that Eid of sacrifice,
tell that light of the Koran,
tell that honour of Rizvan,*
"Drunkards are saluting you."

O our king Hosām al-Din,
O you, the honour of all saints,
O you, the cause of all souls' awareness –
drunkards are saluting you.

ghazal 533

* Rizvan is the doorkeeper of paradise.

A Marble in His Hand

By extolling benevolent qualities of the Divine, Rumi indirectly praises – and perhaps protects – Hosām.

A drunkard is greeting you,
secretly sending a message to you.
The one whose heart you stole
is making his soul your servant too.

O you,
who made non-existence of existence,
hear a greeting from a drunkard –
a drunkard who is willingly caught
in your trap of love.

O sky of lovers,
O soul of lovers' souls,
Your goodness allows you
to succeed among lovers.

O relish of every lip,
O Kabah of every faith,
like a guard,
the moon is circling your roof every night.

He is making physical bodies from dust
and celestial bodies from smoke.
O dust of the body and smoke of the heart,
look how He is transforming you.

One moment He gives you wings,
the next He gives you an anchor.
One moment He makes you day,
the next He makes you night.

One moment He makes you quake,
the next He makes you laugh.
One moment He makes you drunk,
the next He makes you the cup.

You are a marble in His hand –
sometimes the wine,
sometimes drunk on Him.
I swear to God, if He breaks the marble
He is completing you!

Sometimes this, sometimes that –
this will end when you surrender.
Dyeing you with these colours
He is taming you, making you worthy.

For a while, you were fast-paced like Noah.
Now, like a ship, He moves you
without feet or steps.

Stay quiet, sit perplexed.
Be bewildered and cause bewilderment.
You are a man with mature words,
but talk is making you immature.

ghazal 539

The Beloved is Coming

This joyful ghazal may have been composed when Rumi heard of Shams' return to Konya after his first absence.

Splash water on the road,
the beloved is coming!
Give the garden the happy news –
the fragrance of spring is coming.

Make way for the beloved,
for that beauty like the full moon.
From his brilliant light-giving face,
an offering of light is coming.

The sky is splitting in two,
a hubbub is in the world.
Amber and musk are diffusing,
the beloved's banner is coming.

The splendour of the garden is coming,
the eyes and their light are coming.
Sorrow is moving aside,
to our side the moon is coming.

The arrow flies straight to the mark.
Why are we still sitting?
From the hunt, the king is coming.

The garden is welcoming,
the cypress is standing.
By foot, the greenery is arriving.
Mounted, the bud is coming.

I wonder what wine they drink
in the solitude of the sky.
Because the soul is intoxicated and ruined,
with its hangover, wisdom is coming.

When you arrive in our alley,
our nature is to be quiet.
From our talk, only dust is coming.

ghazal 549

The Water of Life is Coming

Choose the inner music over the black water of worldly attraction. The repeated ending phrases provide a steady beat, like a drum.

Pull the cotton from your ears,
the sound of deliverance is coming.
Don't wade into the black water,
the Water of Life is coming.

In the heavens, Jupiter beats his drum
to announce that love is coming.
A hundred blessings
for souls of lovers are coming.

Be entirely milk and honey,
become poor by freeing yourself of your self.
Alms and tithes to the poor
from the King are coming.

By His mercy, those of water and clay
are seeking hearts.
By His pull, fasting and prayers
from humanity are coming.

In the darkness of entanglements,
be patient and accepting.
To Khizr* in the darkness,
the Water of Life is coming.

ghazal 550

* An ancient prophet.

Old Wine in a New Bottle

Famous among Persians, this poem is important because it brings harmony to opposing beliefs held by two groups of Sufis: "Those who believe in rebirth (tanāsukh) hold the view that a soul must go through different forms and lifetimes to purify itself from sins and errors that prevent it from merging in God; those who believe in the oneness of souls (vahdat) say that there is none but one being and all forms are manifestations of that One, but the human form is the only mirror in which God can wholly behold Himself."[146] *Rumi alludes to the oneness of souls, even in transmigration. In the final verse, he refers to himself as the "moon of mystery."*

That red-cloaked one who rose
like the moon last year,
this year in a green cloak has appeared.

That Turk you saw looting last year,
this year in the guise of an Arab has appeared.

His clothing has changed,
but that friend is the same.
He changed his clothing
and has appeared again.

That Wine is the same
though the bottle has changed.
To aid the drunkard,
look at how sweetly He has appeared.

O you, who assumed all torches had died,
in this mysterious window
know that the torch has appeared.

This talk is not about transmigration
but absolute Oneness
which from the swelling of that Sea has appeared.

One drop has separated from that Sea
yet is not separate.
From the potter's clay, Adam has appeared.*

At the time when Habash prevailed,
the Roman concealed himself.†
Today, in this ferocious army he has appeared.

Although the Sun set,
it is not diminished by the sunset.
From another house,
that brilliant moon has appeared.

Leave talk and look through the mirror of your eyes.
From talking, doubts and problems have appeared.

Shams al-Haqq of Tabriz has arrived.
Announce that from the wheel of purity,
the moon of mystery has appeared.

ghazal 639

---

* K 55:14.

† Rumi, as a perfect *murshid*, is the Roman whose light was hidden by darkness or Habash, the name for Ethiopia.

DON'T FIGHT

Make God, not greed, your focus.

Oblivious of destiny, people plan,
but how can that ever be the same
as the fate God commands?

When a limited one ponders,
what he sees is not clear.
He tries to be crafty,
unaware of God's plan.

It looks like he took the proper steps,
but who knows where that leads?

Don't fight.
Seek the domain of love
which will save you
from the angel of death.

Become the King's prey –
don't hunt so much.
The falcon of death
will take back all your quarry.

Be silent and choose a resting place.
The King will place you where you choose.

ghazal 647

The Neighbour

Addressing pilgrims on Hajj, Rumi encourages them to undertake the search for God within the body (house) and to go to the roof (head), bringing a bouquet of roses (spiritual attainments) or a pearl (soul) as a gift for the beloved.

O pilgrims on *hajj*, where are you? Where are you?
Your beloved is here. Come back, come back!

Your beloved is the neighbour who shares your wall.
Why wander in the desert? What are you looking for?

If you see the formless form of the beloved,
you become the Kabah, the house, and its master.

Ten times you traversed the road to that house* –
for once, come up to the roof of this house.

That house is lovely – you described its signs.
Now show me a sign of its master –
show me a bouquet of roses if you see that garden,
show me one pearl of your soul if you come
from God's ocean.

Still, may your troubles be your treasure!
It's a shame you veil your own treasure.

ghazal 648

---

*The Kabah.

Everlasting Wine

Aflāki writes that when Mazhar al-Din, son of Sheikh Seif al-Din Bākharzī, reached Konya, all the important and knowledgeable people of the town went to visit him, showing utmost respect. That same day, Rumi had gone to the mosque with a group of his disciples. Surprised, Sheikh Mazhar al-Din said, "How strange. Hasn't Rumi heard that the 'one who arrives must be greeted'?"

Inside the mosque, explaining inner truth, Rumi said, "O brother, we are the one arriving, not you! You and those like you should come to greet us." Those present at the mosque were bewildered by these words, wondering to whom he was referring. He then gave an example, saying, "When someone comes from Baghdad and another from his own neighbourhood, who is greeted first?" Everyone answered, "The one coming from Baghdad." Rumi responded that, in reality, he had arrived from the Baghdad of No-Place, while this dear son of the Sheikh has come from the domain of this world, so he should be greeting us first. Then he recited this ghazal:[147]

Before grapes, vineyards, or wine in the world,
our* soul was drunk on everlasting Wine.

Before the conflicts and confusion of Mansur,†
we were saying, "I am God"
in the Baghdad of the soul's domain.

Before universal mind started building
with water and dust,
our pleasure and joy blossomed
in the tavern of Truth.

---

* Rumi refers to himself in the third person.
† Mansur was hanged in Baghdad for saying, "I am God" or, more exactly, "I am Truth."

Our soul was like a world,
the cup of the soul like the sun.
In the wine of the soul,
the world was immersed
up to its neck in light.

O *Saqi,* intoxicate those who are proud
of staying in their water and dust,*
so each will know how distant they have been
from such a wealth as yours.

May my life be a sacrifice to that *Saqi*
who comes through the soul
to unveil all that was veiled.

Our mouths fall open before that *Saqi*
who made wine without headache
and nectar without bees.

Keep my mouth closed, O *Saqi* –
otherwise, whatever treasure was hidden
within the seventh earth will be revealed.†

O city of Tabriz,
tell us about that time, if you know,
when Shams-e Din was famous
without Shams-e Din.‡

ghazal 731

---

*The human form.

†K 65:12.

‡When Shams was part of God, before he took human form.

Longing for You

Rumi wants to be in the beloved's presence.

My heart wants you,
passionately longs for you,
and my weary face bears the
sallowness of sorrow over you.

My head is intoxicated by your beauty
and my heart is a trap for your image.
It offers pearls from my eyes
to the bottom of your sea.

I gave every gift I received from you
to your image within,
for your sweet image holds your glory
and looks like you.

I'm wrong!
Your image looks like no other image.
All its goodness and gentle beauty
come from your own bountiful gifts.

The rose dropped all its petals
before you in shame,
for it had assumed it was as beautiful
as your lovely face.

The cypress is downcast,
for it had committed a sin.
It made the mistake of thinking
it was as tall as you.

The hearts and souls of your dear ones
are as bright as Venus.
Yet all are waning like the moon
in longing for you.

My heart is a skillet of halva
on the fire of passion.
If the skillet burns in the blaze,
does it not still hold your sweet halva?

Because you're a friend
you have a seat in every place.
Blessed is the one aware of your place
and unaware of his own.

If you don't open the door for me,
I will enter through the roof
for you are the gentle soul that I long to see.

I will climb onto two hundred rooftops
and will enter two hundred traps.
What can I do? The deer of my soul wants
to graze in your meadow.

Quiet, O mad lover!
Suffer and do not compose poetry.
Every bit of the world has the same
sorrow and turmoil as you.

Go to Tabriz, O heart,
to the virtuous Shams al-Haqq.
When his image comes to you
that means he wants you.

ghazal 759

GRACE AND MIGHT OF LOVE

Rumi speaks of God as Love in its many manifestations.

Laughter tells the story of Your grace
and wailing complains of Your might.
These opposite messages to the world
tell tales of the same Beloved.

Grace can deceive an ignorant one
if he forgets might and commits a crime.
Might can make another feel hopeless,
so he descends into complete despair.

Love, like a gentle comforter,
protects these two who have gone astray.
O God, we are so grateful for this love
that extends limitless grace.

However much we fail to thank You,
Love compensates for our ingratitude.
Is Love a pool of nectar or the Water of Life?

Love makes our lives limitless, boundless.
Like a courier between truth and the accused,
Love runs about, spreading the news.

Stop!
Don't keep analyzing one sign after another.*
Love itself explains the signs.

ghazal 821

* Literally, "*āyat* by *āyat*."

What Else Can It Do?

This ghazal was composed in honour of Salāh al-Din who, at Rumi's behest, dressed like Shams to show the world that Shams was not gone. Shams would always be within Rumi's sight – outside as Salāh al-Din, within as the beloved.

A laughing rose laughs.
What else can it do?
It raises a flag of perfume.
What else can it do?

When a pomegranate's skin cracks open
it laughs, its joy uncontained.
What else can it do?

That brilliant moon
displays beauty and coyness.
What else can it do?

The sun shines and spreads light
over this unique dome.
What else can it do?

The shadow sees
the brilliant face of the sun
and bows and prostrates.
What else can it do?

The lover tears his shirt
over the sweet fragrance of your shirt.
What else can he do?

You pass by a dead body
and it comes to life and moves.
What else can it do?

My heart is like a harp
in the clutches of sorrow over you.
If it can't shout or twang,
what else can it do?

The Lion of God
is King Salāh al-Din.
If he can't roar or hunt,
what else can he do?

ghazal 835

The Peerless Rider*

Aflāki tells us that one day, while Rumi was speaking and all his disciples were present, a devotee entered the madrasa. Rumi welcomed him, saying, "Come in! How good it is that you have come. We have been talking about God and, until now, you have just heard about him from others. From now on, hear directly from God with no mediator. The time comes that God, without a mediator, will be the Sheikh.... This time is such a time." Then Rumi recited this ghazal.[148]

The sun of good fortune
has ascended into the sky again.
The desire of all souls
has arrived through our souls again.

At the pleasure of Rizvan,
the doors of heaven are open again.
Every soul is submerged up to its neck
in the heavenly pool.

That King, the focal point of all kings,
has come again.
That Moon, superior to all moons,
has risen again.

The melancholy have all mounted their horses
because the King, the peerless rider,
has entered the heart of the army.

*Rumi's original composition may have been rearranged in transcription; the sequence of lines 10–13 are reordered to improve the logic of the poem.

Particles of gloomy dust
are astonished and bewildered
upon hearing from the city of No-Place,
"Get up! The resurrection is here."

The causeless Call has come,
not from within or without,
not from front or back,
not from right or left.

You ask, "Where is that coming from?"
From that way you seek and search.

You ask, "Which way then should I turn?"
Towards that way inside your head.
Towards that way where ripeness came to fruit.
Towards that way where stones became gems.
Towards that way where dried-out fish
came to life with Khizr.
Towards that way where Moses' hand
became as luminous as the moon.
Towards that way where a nonbeliever
turns in times of trouble.
Towards that way
where he builds up faith on that side
when faced with pain on this side.

Stay with the pain
so that pain can show you the way –
the way seen by someone
rendered helpless by pain.

The soul has no permission
to reveal this mystery –
otherwise, every nonbeliever
would be free of disbelief.

This burning is like
a brightly lit candle in my heart.
This command is like
a crown of glory on my head.

That great King
has kept the door tightly shut.
Today, He assumed the human form
and came to open it.

Before your sun,
O Shams al-Haqq of Tabriz,
my soul is less than a particle
in absolute humility.

ghazal 841

What Can Remain?

Rhetorical questions paint the beauty of the beloved.

Can a heart ever remain at rest
when your eyes are half open and drunk?*
Can the moon ever compare
to the beauty of your face?

When the minstrel-of-desire-for-you
begins to play his harp of joy,
can Venus remain in business in the heavens?†

When your plundering beauty
moves its army out to strike,
can any town or region be safe in its way?

When your life-extending rose garden
is laughing in my soul's garden,
can roses remain sane,
can a thorn remain a thorn?

When your love, the king,
sends a spy into a heart,
can any friend but love remain in that chest?

What a happy time when suddenly,
by good luck, the soul takes you to its side
and your body remains behind.

---

* Sufis compare the eyes of the *murshid* to the eyes of a drunkard.

† In Sufi literature, Venus is the sky's minstrel and harpist.

When the head is intoxicated
by such an idol,
can the heart seek fortune and fame,
can shame or disgrace remain?

I am begging God
that Shams al-Haqq of Tabriz
will shine in the cave of my heart
and remain with his friend from the cave.*

ghazal 848

* Abū Bakr, friend of the Prophet Muhammad.

The Key

Rending the veil of darkness. Faqr literally means "poverty," but here it refers to the beloved whose poverty does not stem from the state of possessing nothing but rather from knowing that nothing possesses him.

One morning, like morning itself,
the veil of darkness was torn apart.
Suddenly, at midnight, the day of resurrection dawned.

All veils were rent and my self saw Itself.
That which no tongue could speak was heard by no ear.

Your skin will split from joy when love appears,
but the joy felt when He makes you vanish
is beyond compare.

Faqr has taken the lead, ascending level by level.
The auspicious key of *faqr* can open the lock.

One destroyed by passion is filthy, one by wisdom, clean.
Beyond clean and filthy, *faqr* has raised a pavilion.

The hearts of all lovers have circled around *faqr*.
Faqr is the Sheikh of all sheikhs
and all hearts are its disciples.

When my eyes saw my Shams-e Haqq in Tabriz,
He asked, "Are you full now?"
My eyes answered, "Is there any more!"*

ghazal 890

---

* K 50:30.

Scattered Words Have Come

The stages of "union without separation."

Temptations of the body are over
for the uproar from the soul has come.
The ant has gone to its nest
for the banner of Solomon has come.*

How long will this fiery sky stay defiant?
Noah has boarded the ark
for the turmoil of the typhoon has come.

How long will the impotent man
boldly claim to be manly?
Rostam has unsheathed his sword:
Sām and Narimān† have come.

How long will those insignificant conjurers
change canes and ropes into snakes?
Moses and his black snake‡ have come.

The dregs have sunk to the bottom
and the pure have now been released.
The necks of the wolves are broken
for Joseph of Canaan has come.

---

*When Solomon was coming with his vast army, even the ants hid.
† Two characters in the Persian epic, *Shahnameh*.
‡ When Moses threw his staff at God's command, it was transformed into a powerful black snake (*su'bān*) that swallowed the snakes/staffs of Pharaoh's priests (K 7:107–19 and Exodus 7:8–12).

The false dawn has passed
for the day of good fortune has come.
Perishable life has gone –
from the Beloved, eternal life has come.

The suffering of Job and the poverty of Jacob
had no other remedy,
but now mercy from the Merciful has come.

Who fears a thief
when a constable comes to town?
Tell me, who cares about a constable
when a King or Sultan has come?

Behold sincerity without hypocrisy!
Behold union without separation!
Behold the arch and the sound of drums!
I am unique, for "That" has come.

Poetic metre* had checkmated my life.
A life of reading about God has died
for a life of understanding God has come.

The fruit of the heart is ripening
and my soul is enjoying it.
The wind of generosity is beginning to blow –
scattered words have come!

ghazal 895

* Before meeting Shams, Rumi regularly read the works of other poets.

Trail of the Heart

Our hearts provide the way for God to speak to us – we have to go within to find that way.

"Where is my drunken heart going?" I cried.
The Emperor said, "Be quiet! It's coming towards us."

I said, "If you're with me, talking to me inside,
then why is my heart going outside?"

He said, "The heart is ours, our courageous hero,
who wages war with errant thought.

Good luck will follow it wherever it goes.
Say nothing – let it go wherever it wants.
Sometimes, it's an earthly treasure like the sun.
Sometimes, it flies to the sky like a prayer from the Prophet.

Sometimes, it gives the milk of generosity
from the breast of a cloud.
Sometimes, it blows through the rose garden of the soul
like the breeze of dawn.

Follow the trail of the heart to see within
where roses bloom, greenery grows,
and the stream of fidelity flows."

The Builder of worldly forms is simple and formless.
The head and feet of all move without head and feet.*

* The form moves only by the will of the formless.

Even if there is an error, it is still absolutely flawless.
And if there is infidelity, it is still absolutely faithful.

The heart is like a window that illuminates the house.
The body returns to dust – the heart to eternity.
The heart gives rise to troubles and sheds the blood of kings.
It mingles with everyone though it goes alone.

The heart makes the magic of God visible in everyone.
It defeated the Gemini – it goes on like Soha.*
O heart, how foolish it is to keep a secret from you.
The secret is stolen anyway and the soul goes with the thief!

I said, "You are a magician."
He smiled and said, "How can magic be effective?
Remembrance of God goes on and on!"

I said, "Yes, but God's secret is your magic.
Your sweet magic goes with the command of destiny."

The Beloved has constant interaction
with your heart and soul.
You see only what happens in the outer layer.

This heart is like a thirsty horse
drawn to the call of a water wheel.
Outside, the squeak of the wheel scares him away
so his thirst remains unquenched.

ghazal 898

---

*A small star that symbolizes constancy and perseverance in the heart as opposed to Gemini, a symbol of worldly duality.

He Flees from You

The elusiveness of God, His appearance and disappearance in His creation, His inclination to vanish as soon as we get close – all echo the idea of a trickster god.

Hold on to his grace
for he flees so fast.
Don't pull it like an arrow
or he will fly from the bow.

What roles he performs!
What tricks he plays!
While present in his form,
he flees through the soul.

When you seek him in the sky,
he shines like the moon on water.
When you enter the water,
he flees to the sky.

You call him from No-Place
and he shows himself in some place.
You look for him in that place
and he flees to No-Place.

Isn't thought the fastest bird in existence?
Be sure that he surely flees from thought.

I will run from this one and that,
not out of boredom but out of fear –
because my gentle beloved
flees from this and that.

I will run like the wind
for the love of a Rose –
but not for a rose
that runs from the rose garden,
fearful of the autumn wind.

When you begin to say his name,
he flees so fast
that you don't have time
to say, "He will flee!"

He flees from you
so that if you draw his form,
the drawing will flee from the board
and his imprint will flee from your heart!

ghazal 900

Reach the Treasure

A catalogue of impediments to the inner journey which, once undertaken, needs to be in the right direction.

The sky cannot reach
the threshold of mysteries.
A ladder cannot reach
the roof of *faqr* or certainty.

When an *ārif*[*] contemplates
inner knowledge,
a thousand stars or moons
cannot reach his contemplation.

One who becomes an owl[†]
in this ruined world
is separated from nightingales
and cannot reach the rose garden.

Know that a heart
greedy for a grain of silver is cut off
and its soul cannot reach the Mine.

Don't feed your lust with beauties
as if they were fodder.
When your senses are attached to some place
they cannot reach No-Place.

---

[*] A mystic with inner vision.

[†] Among Persians, owls were thought to live among ruins and to bring bad luck.

The deer that is attached to something
will lag behind her friends.
She cannot reach the pleasant pastures
and the tulip beds.

You are going towards Acca*
wanting to reach Mecca.
Don't seek the impossible –
it cannot get you there.

If you put onion and garlic
to your nose and sniff,
you cannot smell
the fragrance of musk.

Be quiet
if you wish to reach
the treasure of consciousness,
for only your heart can reach that,
not your tongue.

ghazal 910

---

* A Syrian port that signifies rebellion.

The Black Lion

Selfless love is both the goal of the path and a trap. Here, Rumi gives us due warning.

Love has stolen my sleep,
love will steal your sleep.
Love won't spend
even half a grain of barley
on life or wisdom.

For love is a bloodthirsty black lion
who drinks nothing
but the blood of lovers' hearts.

Lovingly attaching himself to you,
love leads you into his trap.
Once you are caught, he watches you from afar.

A powerful ruler and a fearless enforcer,
love will torture and strangle the innocent.

Anyone caught in love's grip weeps like a cloud.
Anyone distant from love freezes like snow.

Every moment, love shatters a thousand cups.
Every moment, he sews and rips apart
a thousand garments.

Laughing, love makes a thousand eyes cry profusely.
Killing a thousand people, he sees them as one!

Circling Mount Qāf,
the phoenix flies so effortlessly,
but when it sees the snare of love,
it falls and cannot fly again.

No one can escape his chains
either by madness or deceit.
No wise man can escape his trap by wisdom.

Because of love,
my words are too confusing – otherwise,
I would show you the paths that love treads.
I would show you how love captures the lion.
I would show you how he hunts his prey.

ghazal 919

God Weaves

Leave thought, schemes, and words behind to find the King of Love.

When Love wants to pull you to His side and kiss you,
who can stay calm and relaxed, my dear, who?

The hunting grounds laugh when the King goes hunting,
but what can you say when the King is the hunted?

A thousand cups of wine can't cure my hangover
when my heart is drunk on such drunken eyes.

When I turn to dust, my dust divides, bit by bit –
for isn't my every atom in love with that Beauty?

If you hear a commotion from any flying dust,
know that my every atom is in that dust.

A sigh calms my heart and I feel ashamed.
Even my sigh is ashamed before Your moon-like beauty.

Nothing in the world is better than patience,
but patience while wanting You is a great disgrace.

O you,
sorrowfully pondering this love affair,
unless you leave your self behind there can be no affair.
Stop weaving your web of thoughts like a spider
for the warp and woof are worn out.

Go!
Return that thought to the One who gave it.
Look at the King, not the thought –
that is your offering.

When you stop talking, your talk is His.
When you stop weaving, God weaves.

ghazal 922

Board the Ark

Rumi advises us to fight the mind, the barrier between us and the beloved.

Don't do it, don't do it!
You'll be sorry and that is bad.
Without the gift of a soul
even the garden is like a tomb.

When your body overrules your wisdom,*
why lament?
Why tear your hair in sorrow and regret?

Fight with your mind, fight a bloody war
for such a war promotes peace.

And if you flee
from the lion's claws like a deer,
that moon will flee from you
into the house of the Lion.†

Then your ears won't hear the words
of that kind friend,
and your eyes will not behold
that stately beloved.

Board the ark of the soul
and seize Noah's skirt.
Every moment the tide ebbs and flows
in the ocean of love.

---

* Literally, "pulling wisdom's beard."
† Astrological reference to Leo.

Leave boredom and coyness
for coyness isn't yours.
It belongs only
to that moon-faced beloved.

What an injustice that I compared
his beauty to the moon!
A hundred suns and a hundred skies
are jealous of him.

Be quiet, don't speak, don't count pebbles!
How can the numberless be counted?

ghazal 935

Fly Home

The body is tying us down – let it go!

A call came to souls,
"How long will you stay there?
Come back to your original home.

Because nearness to Us
is your very essence and existence,
fly happily to Mount Qāf for you are a phoenix.*

Water and clay are a heavy log tied to your feet.
Try to untie the log, bit by bit.

Travel back from exile – come home.
Be determined for we are saddened by this separation.

How long will you waste your life
with bitter foul drink, stagnant water,
and wastelands?"

God fashions your wings from your effort.
You are alive – so move and make an effort!

Wings and feathers of hope rot from laziness.
What will you be worth when you lose them?

You are unhappy with freedom,
but not unhappy to be in the pit of this well?
Congratulations – you can remain in the well.

---

*This verse contains two untranslatable word plays to show both oneness and nearness.

Listen to the call,
'O you who have eyes, take warning!'*
You are no longer children –
why do you still chew on your cuffs?

What is the value of seeking, except to find?
Listen! Jump over the stream while you are young!

Why are you crushing water
in the mortar of your passion?
When no water is left, you are just a boastful wind.

God called this hashish-like world 'vainglory.'†
In a world like this, what nonsense are you gnawing on
like an animal?

Hey! The wine has arrived. Come out of the barrel.‡
Refine your bodies for delicious, delightful sweets.

Beware! The beauty of the soul seeks a mirror.
Remove the rust from your mirror by polishing.

They won't let me say all this briefly.
If you are seekers, seek from the Source of the spring.

ghazal 945

---

* K 59:2.
† K 57:20.
‡ The physical body.

A Star Shines Within You

The Beloved is everywhere. If we cannot perceive Him, it is because our own choices make us unaware.

Where is one mouth from which
the fragrance of the soul is not coming?
Where is one heart to which
that Sign is not coming?

What is every particle of the universe
chewing on like a camel
if a morsel from that renowned Banquet
is not coming?

Why are the dogs of greed
pacing from left to right
if the smell of fried food from that Pot
is not coming?

Why are the lions' paws
quivering like flower petals
if into all hearts spears from the Unseen
are not coming?

Why are a thousand lambs and wolves
eating from the same pasture
if into their lives, the power and voice
of the shepherd are not coming?

Without ears, the soul hears two hundred shouts.
Listen and be attentive
even if to you they are not coming.

Why would new life ever begin
in this old world
if at every moment, support from
the other world is not coming?

You scatter dust over your own eyes
with your own hands
to convince yourself
that new faces are not coming.

Look at the life spans
of a hundred thousand long-lived kings
like Zulgurnain* as lost time.
Though many are close to God,
to them the fortunate invincible One
is not coming.

Has anyone cleansed his hands and mouth
with the Water of fidelity
into whose mouth, breath after breath,
the Wine of the soul is not coming?

Has anyone taken a few steps towards
the rose garden of love
to whom a hundred salutations
from that Gardener are not coming?

* Literally, "the one with two horns." Refers to a king, usually Alexander the Great.

Beyond love
there are thousands and thousands of porticos
so grand and glorious to the imagination
that are not coming.

Every moment
a Star shines within you, saying,
"Look! Don't say that a sign from the sky
is not coming."

Close your mouth
and the creator of the mouth
will describe it in a way that,
to your tongue, is not coming.

ghazal 958

He Baked Me Thoroughly

After the transformation of the disciple into the lover comes the inner journey – upwards, always upwards.

Your love made me drunk, made me clap my hands.
Drunk and unaware of myself, what can I do?

Once a sour grape, now I am sweet.
I cannot make myself sour again.

The halva-selling friend, sweet as sugar,
placed a handful of halva in my mouth.

When he opened a halva shop,
he took over my house and my shop as well!

People are saying, "You should not be that way!"
I wasn't like this – he made me this way.

First, he broke my barrel and poured out the vinegar.
I lamented that he caused me loss.

Then, in place of that, he made me happy
with hundreds of barrels of Wine.

In his oven of misfortune and suffering,
he baked me thoroughly like crusty bread.

In sorrow, I grew old like Zulaikhā,*
until Joseph's prayers made me young again.

---

*Zulaikhā tried to seduce Joseph; when he rejected her, she falsely accused him of attempted rape (K 12:23–9 and Genesis 39:12).

Like an arrow, I flew from his hand.
Then he seized me and turned me into a bow.

I will fill earth and sky with gratitude
for, though I was earth, now I am sky.

My heart passed through stars and constellations,
then he pulled me beyond all the galaxies.

I saw many ladders and roofs,
then he freed me from roofs and ladders.

Once my story filled the world,
he hid me in the world like a soul.

When he found that I was as soft as a tongue,
he made me interpret like a tongue.

Because I was connected to the heart like a tongue,
he told me the heart's secrets, one by one.

When my tongue began to shed blood,
he sheathed me in a scabbard like a sword.

Enough, O heart! All that my loving friend did
cannot be described by the tongue.

ghazal 971

Candlelight

Some habits necessary for a spiritual life.

Patience doesn't suit love.
Wisdom cannot help at all.
Selflessness is a joyful realm,
but no one can rule over it.

Though the caravan of life is passing by,
no sound of bells comes at all.
Though the rose garden's fragrance
invites you to the rose,
no desire comes to you at all.

Because a very active mind fills you,
this fragrant breath* can't come to you.
Without a masterful, gentle God
honey cannot come from a fly.

With every breath, plant a seed of goodness.
Without planting seeds, a harvest cannot come.
Have you ever had a good thought
from which a reward did not come?

Stop, for this candlelight of talk
does not come into every darkness.†

ghazal 989

*The word for "breath" (*nafas*) is a pun on the Arabic and Persian word for "self" or "mind" (*nafs*).

† Rumi uses a term for the hours just before dawn.

Look at the Giver

Focus on the essential, not the trivial.

Look at the *Saqi,* don't look at the drunkard.
Look at Joseph, don't look at your hands.

O soul, you're a fish caught on the hook of a body.
Look at the fisherman, don't look at the hook.

Look at the soul that you were in the beginning.
Don't look at the body that has joined you now.

Look at that rose garden without end.
Don't look at the thorn that has pierced your foot.

Look at the Phoenix casting his shadow on you.
Don't look at the crow that flew out of your hand.

Strive ever upwards like the cypress and hyacinth.
Don't look at the ground like the violet.

When the Water of Life starts to flow in your stream,
don't look at the barrel or jug* if it breaks.

Look at the Giver of life, the Giver of bliss.
Don't look at existence and don't cry for non-existence.

* The body and heart.

Look at contentment that's virile and light.
Don't look at greed that's pregnant and slow.

Look at the pure who rose to the top.
Don't look at the dregs that have sunk to the bottom.

Look at the world filled with heavenly faces.
Don't look at the one who blocked your way.

Wondrous birds are caught in the trap of love.
Don't look at the owl that escaped love's snare.

A better speaker than you is waiting in ambush.
Don't look at the fact that he's quiet right now.

ghazal 1044

Remember!

A love story well known among Persians expresses Rumi's agony of separation from Shams. Khusro was a Sāsānid king of Persia who loved Shirin, the crown princess of Armenia. Farhād, an architect, was also in love with Shirin. To remove his rival, Khusro commissioned Farhād to carve a stream from the top of the granite mountains miles away to Shirin's bath in the palace so she could bathe every morning in the fresh milk from the flock of sheep grazing there. Farhād did it. Khusro then ordered him to carve some stairs on the same granite mountains. He was certain that Farhād could not finish this work, so he promised Shirin to him when the project was complete. When Khusro finally realized that Farhād's love would accomplish the impossible, he sent a messenger to give him false news of Shirin's death. On hearing this, Farhād hit himself on the head with the same tool he was using to chip away the mountain and died.

You resolved to leave like sweet life – remember!
You saddled the horse of separation despite us – remember!

Over earth and sky true friends gather around you,
but you swore an oath to this old friend – remember!

I erred and that caused you unhappiness.
But remember our nights, O beloved,
you who are without resentment – remember!

Every night when you lay your moon-like face on the pillow
remember that you used my lap as your pillow – remember!

Like Farhād, in desire
I chip away at the mountain of our separation.
Oh, Khusro and a hundred like Shirin
are your slaves – remember!

You have seen the desert of love at the seashore of my eyes,
filled with shoots of saffron and narcissus – remember!

My fiery pleading rises skyward.[*]
Gabriel, next to God's throne,
says, 'Amen!' – remember!

Shams-e Tabrizi, since the first day I saw your face
my religion has been love for your face.
O honour of religion – remember!

ghazal 1063

---

[*] K 19:3–4.

ORBIT OF LOVE

The physical form of Shams is no longer with him, but Rumi has achieved complete absorption in the beloved and sees the light of Shams everywhere.

Moment after moment,
the king appeared from behind the veil,
then again he was veiled.
Eight times this happened.

For an hour, he stole the hearts and wisdom
of those outside.
For an hour, he struck the residents
of the inner sanctum unconscious.

A book of sorcery lay open before his eyes
and the hearts of the restless
were moved by the movement of his eyes.

Sometimes, melancholy drew his form
with the tip of its pen.
Sometimes, poor wisdom was stoned to death
by the sound of the oboe of his love.

When night fell,
his face glowed like a candle
and two hundred moth-like souls
orbited around it.

Halfway through the night,
the drunkards fell unconscious.
Only I remained with the night,
the candle, the wine, and that beauty.

My "me" was also asleep,
no longer causing trouble.
My "Me" sat side by side with his "Me."*

At dawn,
when my "me" was eager for that "Me,"
my "me" entered like a shadow
and the beloved's "Me" departed.

Shams-e Tabrizi is gone,
but the radiance of his face
shines light in every direction
to whomever he wants.

ghazal 1076

* "Me" refers to the soul and "me" to the mind/ego.

The Cypress

His heart filled with joy and laughter, Rumi describes the unity that springs from divine love.

I sense the beloved's fragrance
with every breath,
so how could I not embrace myself
every night?

Last night in the garden of love,
passion coursed through my head.
Love for him sprang from my eyes
and a river began to flow.

Every laughing rose
blooming on the riverbank of love
has fled the thorns of existence
and the jagged sword of death.*

Each tree and blade of grass
in the meadow was dancing
although, to the passerby,
they seemed rooted in place.

Suddenly,
our cypress appeared out of nowhere.
The garden grew ecstatic
and the plane tree applauded.

* The sword of Ali.

Face, Wine, and Love like fire –
all three full of joy.
Surrounded by fire the soul wails,
wanting to flee.

In the world of divine Union,
who needs numbers?
But they must exist
in the world of five and four.*

Count a hundred thousand sweet apples by hand.
Crush them together to make them one.[149]

Veiled by skin, grapes number a hundred thousand.
Without skin, only royal Wine remains.

Look! Without words,
what is this talk in the heart?
It's a colourless colour and a formless form
rising from the Essence.

Shams-e Tabrizi is seated as king.
Before him, my verses line up like chosen slaves.

ghazal 1077

* Five senses, four elements.

Get Out of the Bath

The world as a public bath where souls are sent to be washed clean of attachment.

That idol gave me a broom and said,
"Raise dust from the sea!"

Then he set that broom ablaze and said,
"Bring me a broom from the fire."

Perplexed, I bowed before him.
He said, "Without bowing, give a good bow."

Ah, how can there be bowing
without someone bowing?
He said, "Without questioning or complaining."

I bent my head before him and said,
"Cut off this head with your sword."

The more he struck, the more heads grew
'til a hundred thousand heads had grown
from my neck.

I was a lamp and each head a wick,
set ablaze all around.

Candles appeared from my heads,
in rows from east to west.

What is east or west in the land of No-Place?
It's a hot, dark furnace beneath a working bath.*

O you, with your cold nature,
where is the restlessness in your heart?
How long will you stay in this hot bath?

Get out of the bath and don't go into the furnace.
Get dressed and look at the paintings and décor.

Behold the heart-ravishing images
and see the colours of the tulip bed.

Then, look up towards the window.
That idol became an idol from his image reflected there.

The six directions are the bath,
the window is No-Place and, above the window,
the king's face comes into view.

Earth and water are full of colour from his reflection.
He has showered life on everyone.

The day is gone but my story still is long.
Oh, how night and day are shamed over his long story.

The king, Shams al-Din of Tabriz,
keeps me drunk, round after round.

ghazal 1095

---

* The dark furnace refers to the fire below a Roman-style public bath.

Secret Pearls

Rumi is totally intoxicated, totally absorbed in the light of the Sun.

If you are aware of the mystery of his love,
give your life to love and gaze at the beloved.

Love is a sea, its waves invisible.
Sea water is like fire, its waves like pearls.

The pearls are secrets, whose every facet
leads a wayfarer to inner meaning.

You will leave the two worlds completely
if you learn even an iota of this mystery.

Last night I was drunk, asleep at midnight
when that moon passed by.

In the moonlight, he saw my sallow face.
His tears poured and wet my face.

Out of his mercy, he gave me the nectar of union.
My body, hair by hair, found new life.

Although I was totally drunk on Wine,
my hairs, one by one, began to see.

Absolutely drunk, I kept looking
at the face of that Sun of existence.

ghazal 1096

Love is the Best Ladder

Love brings pain that can be endured only by a warrior.

Wisdom is a chain holding the wayfarer back, O son.
Break the chain for the way is visible, O son.

Wisdom is a shackle, the heart deceit, and life a veil.
The path is hidden from all three, O son.

Once you give up heart, wisdom, and life,
that certainty is also uncertain, O son!

A man not free from himself is not a man.
Love without pain is a fairy tale, O son.

Make your chest a target for the friend,
whose arrow is certainly eager in the bow, O son.

When your chest is afflicted by the wound of his arrow,
a hundred marks show on your face, O son.

Love is not a task for the soft and tender.
Love is a task for a hero, O son.

Whoever becomes a devotee of lovers
is a king with great good fortune, O son.

Don't ask about love from anyone but love.
Love is a pearl-pouring cloud, O son.

Needless of my translation,
love interprets itself, O son.

If you want to climb to the seventh sky,
love is the best ladder, O son.

Wherever you see a caravan heading,
love is its direction,* O son.

Don't be deceived by the loving kindness
of this world, for this world will leave you, O son.

Now close your mouth and stay quiet like an oyster
for your tongue is the enemy of your soul, O son.

The Sun of Tabriz has arrived and the soul is happy
because it is in the same house as his sun, O son.†

ghazal 1097

---

* Literally, "*qibla*," the direction towards which Muslims pray.

† "The same house" is an astrological reference tied with Shams' name, meaning "sun."

Look at His Face

Lovers, wretched in their separation, are always ready to buy what love offers.

Gently, softly, look at his face.
Open your eyes and see his drunken eyes.
When that priceless ruby laughs,
look at how he captivates
a hundred thousand hearts.
Leave drunkenness. Wake up!
Look at what he has done
and the fortune he received from wakefulness.

Enter the endless garden of the heart.
Look at its abundant, sweet fruits.
Look at its dancing, green branches.
Look at its elegant roses, free of thorns.
How long will you gaze at the face of the world?
Turn around and see its mysteries.

Look at the greedy nature of plants and animals.
Then look at their generosity and contentment.
Both greed and contentment are skills of Love.
If you haven't seen Love, look at His handiwork.
If you haven't seen the mixer of Love's colours,
see the colour of His wretched lovers' faces.
Despite the difficult market He has,
see His buyers, both with and without gold.

ghazal 1101

Needlessness

When you have the beloved, there are no other needs.

What has love to do with talking or hinting?
What has the soul to do with faces and names?

A lover is like a ball, struck by the friend's polo stick.
What has a ball to do with hands and feet?

Wherever His polo stick propels it, it goes.
What has a ball to do with ups and downs?

The mirror reflects the faces of idols.
What has it to do with beautiful or ugly?

The lizard doesn't need to drink water.
What has it to do with a spring of water?

That image resides in the consciousness.
What need has it for here or there?

Jesus passed beyond the heavens.
What worry does he have about hot or cold weather?

O you,
who sing songs with the Invisible Musician, go!
What have you to do with talking and tumult?

ghazal 1102

Patience

Patience is impossible in the presence of the beauty of the inner beloved.

Oh, thoughts of you stroll in my heart
every dawn like the moon in full light.

In my soul, your sweet form creates
fire and passion – what passion!
You lit a fire, saying, "Be patient!"
I don't know how to be patient in an oven.

Remember last night
when you came here drunk?
Were you a moon, a fairy,
or the essence of heavenly beauty?
The words you uttered, sweet as sugar.
The gestures you made, from a distance.

Touching your cheek, you meant,
"For the sake of my heart, don't be anxious!"
Putting your finger to your lips, you meant,
"Have patience!"
How can I be patient with your ruby lips?
Looking up, you meant,
"O God, protect my beauty from evil eyes!"

Oh, you are devoid of any form, yet on your face,
Joseph manifests every moment.

ghazal 1105

Clinging

From doubt and indecision to the joy of the unveiled soul.

The heart sees Your beauty and still waits?
The soul is drunk on Your rose garden
and still doubts?

Every moment,
His radiant glance at my heart
puts an idol on my left
and a beauty on my right.

Every dawn,
when the snare of morning and night breaks,
a kiss comes from the friend
and we begin a hundred thousand prostrations.

Although the last year spent in this love
will not come back,
there is still a circle of impassioned lovers
this year.

Play undying melodies on the harp of love,
for my soul is threadbare
from the firm grip of Your love.

In desire for Your love
and by the radiance of life,
the tree has established roots
and will bear fruit.

The soul dives to the bottom of the sea
and becomes a pearl.
The sea and this pearl
are longing for Your Ruby.

Your sugar-eating parrot* sings songs
and the willow branches dance,
and the maple leaves clap.

After an argument over purity
the Sufis of love
embrace each other like drunkards.

Drunk on the oneness of *Alast,*†
the souls leapt out
without rest or tranquillity
like a torrent towards the sea.

Shot like an arrow from the Essential bow,
the soul aims at nothing
and lands on nothing but the Essential.

This joyful soul is unveiled
from a hundred thousand coverings.
Now it enjoys eternal pampering.

All the sincere souls in love
now cling to Him to gain fortune
from that celebrated Soul.

---

* The egoless soul.

† K 7:172; literally, "am I not [your Lord]." Refers to the covenant with God.

He is the axis[*]
and the souls seize his skirt with love –
and, with courage and strength,
he seizes the skirt of the Absolute Eternal.

Go to Tabriz, O heart,
and ask about this from Shams-e Haqq.
Then you can mount the Burāq[†]
of the secret of meanings.

ghazal 1117

[*] Sufi spiritual leader (*qutb*).
[†] The horse ridden by the Prophet Muhammad during his ascent (*mi'rāj*).

The Baker

The mysterious creation: one day God will tell us His purpose.

Stop thinking and don't hold thoughts in your heart,
for you are naked – and thinking is as cold as ice.

You keep thinking about how to be saved
from sickness and pain,
but thinking is the very source of sickness.

Know that the market of creation is beyond thought.
Read the signs, O you who are ridiculed by true knowledge.

See that lane from which all images fly.
See that stream that makes the old wheel turn.
See that rosy cheek that makes the heart-stealers' cheeks rosy.
See that source of trouble that turns the faces of lovers sallow.

A hundred thousand birds fly joyfully from No-Place.
A hundred thousand arrows are shot from one bow.

Beyond traditions and comprehension,
beyond the why and how,
the Unseen is kneading, without hands,
a hundred thousand batches of dough.

Without fire, He has kindled
ovens of stomachs and hearts.
In the shop, the bread is on display
but our Baker is hidden.

He makes a hundred thousand images
from a simple slate of dust.
He gives a hundred thousand urns of milk
from the heat of mothers' blood.

All you did was beg in God's name
and the call came from the sky,
"Open your basket, O supplicant, the gift is coming."

That morsel was so heavy it tore your basket –
from God's kitchen, there are no small gifts.

He sends manna and quail* from the sky.
He pulls a creature out of a mountain crevice.
He creates the hero Rostam from one drop of semen.
He creates a way for the sleeper to fly while asleep.

Every moment He makes an image in No-Place
that will quickly find its way to the creation.

I follow His command and stop because He said, "Stop."
Someday, that Ruler will illuminate this for you.

ghazal 1122

---

* K 2:57.

Enslaved by That Melody

The sweet melody of the Water of Life.

A melody is sweet if, afterwards,
the reflection of that idol's sun-like face can be seen.

He rises like the sun, and the particle becomes restless,
saying, "Don't keep that spring-like face behind a veil."

Rise, this is our day, our heart-illuminating day!
Love is glowing from our longing.

Rise! We are saved – we have broken our chains.
Rise! We are eternally drunk without a hangover.

Rise, for the soul has come,
the soul and the world have come.
Clapping his hands, he has come.
O heart, do something!

The Water of Life has come.
The day of salvation has come.
Sugar and sweets have come.
O idol, you rain sweets!

I am enslaved by that melody
but pretended to be deaf,
so the chamberlain would whisper in my ear.

When he saw through my trick,
he cooked up his own –
he bit my ear and said, "Hey, you charlatan!"

Rudeness is also good
if it engages him in a war.
I will not turn away from the friend
because of such give and take.

This life is your war, because it is fleeting.
Your war is sweet as sugar.
Your peace? Don't even ask!

ghazal 1123

Love Has Showered Gold

Rumi tells us the importance of divine love in our lives – and its transformative power.

Don't give value to a life lived without love.
Accept love – the Water of Life –
into your heart and soul.

Anyone other than a lover
is nothing but a fish out of water.
Even if he is a vizier, he is dead and withered.

When love spreads its garment,
every tree turns green.
With every breath, a young leaf
sprouts from an old branch.

When could love's prey
ever become death's prey?
When his shield is the moon,
how could an arrow wound him?

When you turned away from God,
did you find another way?
Come back – don't go in vain,
stubbornly, stubbornly.

Buy the calamity He offers as a jar of sugar –
otherwise, you will stay like vinegar.
Fall in love with this ruler –
otherwise, go and die.*

---

*A pun on *mīr* (ruler) and *bimīr* (die).

Pure souls have all become slaves to dust.*
Love has showered gold to free those slaves.

O you, into whose basket
no one else has put any bread,
seek it at the bottom of your own basket, O *faqir*.†

Be swift, strong, and courageous
and God will give you a hundred gifts –
black dust becomes gold,
black blood becomes milk.

Come! Shams al-Haqq,
the honour of the people of Tabriz,
free the heart's feet
from the tar-like dust and water!

ghazal 1129

* The body.
† A mystic or seeker.

SURRENDER

Love will confound and confuse us until we surrender.

The Beloved won't let you stay
loyal or disloyal,
in acceptance or in denial.

Wherever you put your heart,
He will pull it disapprovingly,
so don't put yourself anywhere, O heart –
and don't insist.

You decide on something at night,
He changes it in the morning.
Learn the lesson from changes
between day and night.

In ignorance, the neglectful make promises
of repentance and oath-taking.
What wiles can the submissive use
in the hands of the dominant?

O brother, don't you know
who you're dealing with?
He's the One who makes the whirling dome
circle without head and feet.*

O brother, why are you sleeping?
Don't you know that a wakeful viper
sits coiled on your head?

* Means both "without its own motive force" and "intoxicated."

What dreams are you having,
O proud heart?
Don't you know what dishes
the old Chef has prepared for you?

Following the scent of profit,
a thousand merchants went travelling –
the power of God's command
made their souls restless.

It made them unable to stay in cities
and, bored by the desert, they went to the sea.

When they went to find coral,
it cost them their lives –
along the way, an assassin was lying in ambush.

They ran after Water
and found nothing but a mirage.
They ran after Light
and found nothing but fire.

Destiny grabbed their ears,
tugging, tugging, saying, "Come!"
This is how donkeys
are pulled towards their load.

You are worse than an ox –
to keep you circling,
your neck is tied to a wheel you can't see.

Physicians are also caught in this circling,
because their patients
are drunk and sick from circling.

They are pulled to land, to sea,
to mountain and prairie,
where the claws of the hunting lion
can tear them apart.

But when the lion tears apart a lover of God,
hey, don't think that is the same
as tearing others apart!

When he finds no heart and no liver
in the lover's body,
the dismembering lion[*] becomes a rebuilder.

The lover died miserably at the hands of love,
following the command, 'Die before your death.'[†]

Certainly he is a lover, for his heart is gone
and his liver is smeared in blood.[‡]
No lion will devour prey already killed.

---

[*] There is a parable in the *Masnavi* in which a lion kills a donkey but finds neither liver nor heart.
[†] A hadith.
[‡] The liver is considered the seat of emotions.

And if by mistake the lion did,
he would repair it immediately.
He would breathe the breath of life into him
and hold him to his side.

Eating meat and fat from a lover
is forbidden by God,
so the man-eating lion
would not seek him as prey.

Go on drinking love,
for it is the special antidote to poison*
and the poison dares not inflict any harm.

The talk turned to love
and my heart skipped a beat.
Where can a string run
from such a daring pluck?

When the axis cannot escape
from amid the circling heavens,
tell me, where can a point escape
from such a Compass?

Silence, for this also is destiny's challenge.
You are involved with silk and satin,
and I, with poetry.

ghazal 1133

---

*The poison of ignorance.

The Collapsing House

The body is a decaying house, reminding us that time is short.

Why won't even one in this caravan wake up?
Whose garment of life will the swindler* take now?

Why not hurt sleep and the swindler?
Why hurt the one who gives you awareness?

The one who hurts you
is your sheikh and your adviser,
because love for the world
is like painting on water.

Secretly, a man repeatedly told his house,
"Don't suddenly collapse.
Let me know beforehand."

One night the house suddenly fell on him.
And what did he say?
"What happened to all my pleadings?

Didn't I tell you to let me know
before collapsing,
so my wife and I could escape?

You didn't let me know, O house,
what happened to honouring my wishes?
You fell on me and killed me so wretchedly!"

*Death.

The house answered clearly,
"Day and night, I let you know.
I opened my mouth as a crack
telling you that my strength
was exhausted, beware!
With handfuls of mud
you kept covering my mouth.
Being greedy, you just concealed
the cracks in my walls.
Wherever I opened my mouth,
you closed it and did not let me speak.
What else can I say, O builder?"

Know your body is the house
and your pains are the cracks.
You cover your cracks of pain with medication.

Like a plaster of straw and mud
is that phoney medicine.
Hey! Just press the plaster into the crack!

The body has opened its mouth
to say, "I am dying."
The physician comes and closes its mouth.

The wine of death is the cause
of your drunken headache.
Put down the pomegranate wine
and don't drink that violet extract!*

---

* Plant extracts used as therapy.

Taking it out of habit is just a cover-up.
What can you conceal from the Knower of all secrets?

Drink the wine of returning to God.
Swallow the pill of abstinence.

Blend a potion of repentance.
Make begging for forgiveness your food.

Take the pulse of your faith and heart
to see how you are.
For once, inspect the chamber pot* of your action.

Take refuge in God, He holds the Water of Life.
Be careful! Ask His protection with every breath.

If someone says, "It's not useful to ask,"
say, "If it is His will to ask,
how could it have no effect?"

In Arabic *murīd* means one who wants.
Murīd belongs to *Murād*,†
as the hunted to the hunter.

"If he didn't want me,
then what made me want him?
My face has become sallow
in separation from that face.

---

* Inspecting a urine sample was standard medical practice.
† The sheikh; literally, "the desired."

If his amorous gaze didn't wound me
with its dagger of love,
why is my heart bathed in blood
and why do my eyes shed tears of blood?

Autumn – yellow and sighing –
is the *murīd* of spring.
Won't help from the sheikh of spring
finally come?

If the *murīd* of spring came to life,
why then would the *murīd* of God
remain lifeless and cast aside?"

Come to the garden
and see the result of action.
Blossoms worthy of every pure seed
are on display.

Like the green-robed preachers of spring,
O soul, speak with the tongue of your state
and stay quiet, O friend.

ghazal 1134

The Wine of Love

Aflāki says that one day a group of ārifān went to visit Rumi, and one of them asked about a hadith where it mentions the Wine given by almighty God to his saints; he wanted to know the nature of this Wine.

Rumi said, "When Muhammad reached a particular inner state, with the inner eye he beheld the beauty and power of the Glorious One. After Muhammad's discovery of gentle divinity and after investigating the secrets of the divine treasures, two world-illuminating cups appeared from God's exalted threshold: one full of pure wine and one full of energizing milk. He was invited to choose one.

"The Prophet said, 'I choose the milk and leave the wine for the saints among my people.' He kept the cup of Truth for the ārifān among his people. It is by the sweet fragrance of that wine that perfect saints can lose themselves sometimes and discover the secrets."

Rumi continued, "Which sweet drink did the son of Adham drink that he was drunkenly disgusted with kingdom and country? What intoxication declared, 'May I be praised?' What made Hallāj say, 'I am God' only to be hanged on the gallows?" and then composed the following poem to further answer the question.[150]

Bring a cup for the soul, O *Saqi*, from wherever you can.
May my head and turban be a sacrifice to you!

Enter drunk and strolling, cup in hand.
Don't let us stay sober with a *Saqi* like you.

Bring that cup, in desire for which even my life left,
not to mention my patience and poise!

Bring that life-giving cup that is like your own nature –
intimate of weary hearts, confidant of secrets.

If just a sip is poured from that Wine,
a rose garden will spring instantly from a salt marsh!

If the ruby Wine begins bubbling at midnight,
it will fill the sky with light!

What a Wine, what a cup, what a *Saqi*!
To them, may lives and souls be a sacrifice – a sacrifice!

Come! Many secrets are hidden in my heart.
Pass the ruby Wine and let no veil remain!

When you make me drunk,
then see how a hunter of lions acts among the prey.

Praise God!
The moment the assembly is filled with the cup's aroma
and the light from the face of that Beloved,
a thousand drunks, like moths around a candle,
put their lives on a tray, meaning,
"Take these and give us that."

With the sweet singing of musicians
and the shouting of drunkards,
the Wine changes its behaviour in the drinker's veins.*

Look what it did to those youths in the cave!
They remained dead drunk
for three hundred and nine years.†

---

* Makes the drinker sober, more aware.

† A story in the Koran in which several young people were persecuted for their belief in God. Guided by God, they fled and hid in the cave of *Kahf*. They fell asleep for 309 years and awoke to find themselves in a society that accepted God (K 18:9–26).

What did Moses pour on the magicians
to intoxicate them?
Unaware of their hands and feet,
they all fell drunk and unconscious.*

What did the Egyptian women see in Joseph's face
that they cut their own beautiful hands?

What did the *Saqi* pour on St. George's head
to sanctify him, that he was neither sad nor afraid
of the pagans' fire?†

They killed him a thousand times,
but he kept moving forward, saying,
"I am drunk and not aware of a thousand or one!"

The companions of the Prophet
who went to war without armour
were dead drunk from Muhammad's love.‡

That is wrong! Muhammad was not the *Saqi*,
he was a cup filled with Wine.
God was the *Saqi* for the pious ones.

Which sweet drink did the son of Adham drink
that he was drunkenly disgusted
with kingdom and country?§

---

* K 20:63–73.
† St. George was executed because of his refusal to submit and sacrifice to Roman gods.
‡ Hadith: "O Allah's apostle, what makes Allah laugh with joy at his servant?" He answered, "When he plunges into the midst of the enemy without mail."
§ Adham was a king who renounced his kingdom to live as an ascetic.

What intoxication declared, "May I be praised?"*
What made Hallāj say, "I am God"
only to be hanged on the gallows?

By the aroma of this Wine,
the water became pure and bright,
staggering like a drunk and prostrating before the sea.

By love for this Wine, dust has become colourful.
By the glow of this Wine, fire burns with glowing cheeks.

Without Wine,
why would the wind become a companion and storyteller,
the life of greenery and flower gardens, and a book of tales?

When they mingled,
what fervour did the four elements have
that caused humans, animals, and plants to emerge?

What consciousness-stealing Wine does the black night have
that made people motionless with just one cup?

Which grace or craft of the Creator should I mention?
The sea of His power has invisible shores.

We will drink the Wine of love and carry the load of love
like a drunken camel in a caravan.

---

* In his ecstasy, Bāyazīd Bastāmī exclaimed, "May I be praised, how great is my station!"

Not drunkenness to make you desire sobriety,
but drunkenness that awakens your soul and wisdom.

We will vomit all we have except God
because everything else is a headache and a hangover.

How can pure Wine be compared to wine from grapes?
The pure is the Water of Life, the other a carcass.

One moment it makes you like a monkey,
the next like a pig.
With such red water,
you finally become black-faced, disgraced.

The heart is a barrel of God's Wine – open it at the top!
Your ill-mannered nature has covered the top with mud.

When you remove just a bit of mud from the barrel top,
fragrance flows out and a hundred thousand signs appear.

If I attempt to count the signs of this Wine,
it won't be possible – even by the day of reckoning.

Because we are helpless, we stop with, 'do not count.'*
When it's time to stop, we take up the cup of the soul.

Enter the assembly of lovers of the Sun of Tabriz,
for this Sun takes its light from that Sun.†

ghazal 1135

* A hadith.
† A pun on Shams.

A Sour Morsel

Rumi uses a gently scolding tone to condemn human greed.

Around the face of the beloved
God has written a line that says,
'Learn from it, O you who have eyes.'*

Because love is a man-eater,
man must make himself into a morsel for love.

You are a sour morsel, hard to digest.
The saint is a sweet, pleasing, and wholesome morsel.

Break yourself apart, O morsel – that mouth is small.
It would take three elephants three meals to consume you!

Compared with your greed,
the elephant is a mere morsel.
You are like the swallow that hunted an elephant.

You were born from non-existence
with long-lasting hunger.
Chicken, snake, or scorpion –
all dishes are the same to you!

You reach for a hot pot
and sometimes it burns your mouth –
sometimes it turns your lips, turban,
and garment black.†

---

* K 59:2 commands, 'Learn, O you who have eyes.' Rumi has added two words.
† This stanza alludes to clerics who make a living by representing God and religion without true knowledge of God.

Like the stomach of hell,
nothing will fill you up[*]
unless the powerful Creator steps on you.
When He steps on hell,
hell yells, "I'm full. Take your foot off me!"

God is the one who satiates
the eyes of saints and special ones
for they are free from self and
free from greed for this carcass.[†]

Neither greed for knowledge and art
nor greed for paradise is left in them.
They seek no camel or donkey
for they are mounted on a lion.

Quiet! If I count His favours and gifts,
the count will daze and confuse
the day of reckoning.[‡]

Come, you honour of Tabriz,
the true Shams-e Din, Sun of religion –
the sun of the whirling dome
is your least important servant.

ghazal 1136

---

[*] K 50:30.
[†] The world.
[‡] Play on the words *shumār* (means "counting or calculating") and *rūz-i shumār* (means "day of reckoning").

Contrary is the Beckoning of Love

Love is the killer but lovers go to their death willingly, even as it takes everything they have.

How much suffering
I endured from the beloved
until my bleeding heart and weeping eyes
confirmed this endeavour.

A thousand fires, sighs, and sorrows exist –
their name is love.
A thousand pains, regrets, and troubles exist –
their name is beloved.

Anyone who is an enemy of his own life
is welcome.
You're invited to give your life,
to be killed miserably.

Look at me,
for his worth is a hundred times more
than all I am saying.
I am not afraid. I will not run away
from the beloved who's killing me.

Like the water of the Nile,
the torture of love has two sides –
as water to its own people
and as bloodsucker to others.

If the incense and candle don't burn,
what are they worth?
Unlit, there is no difference
between a heap of twigs and incense.

If dagger, arrow, or spear do not wound in war,
what is the difference
between the unmanly and Rostam, the hero?

To Rostam, that dagger is sweeter than sugar.
Arrows shot at him are the most delectable of gifts.

This lion captures his prey
with two hundred amorous gestures!
Desiring him, the hunted run after him in legions.

Smeared in blood, the dead prey begs inside,
"For God's sake, kill me one more time!"

The eyes of the dead gaze at the living
and say, "O you, ignorant and withered,
come without delay!"

Quiet, quiet –
for contrary is this beckoning of love.
Meanings will hide with too much talk.

ghazal 1138

Don't Squeeze the Sugar Cane

Rumi expresses joy.

We have returned like the spring breeze.
We have risen like the sun
with overflowing confidence.

We are like the July sun
despite the winter season.
We have spread joy and happy songs
in the flower garden.

A thousand ringneck doves are seeking us,
singing, "Coo, coo, coo."*
A thousand nightingales and parrots
are flying towards us.

When fish in the sea received news of us,
a thousand waves boiled from the sea.

I swear on the essence of that God
who gives intelligence and the five senses
that we will leave no wise person
sober in the world.

I swear to Mustafā and his four wise friends
that they will play five times for us in the mysteries.†

---

* In Persian, *coo* means "Where?"
† Playing a drum five times in front of a palace acknowledged the king's power.

We are coming from Egypt with
two hundred camel trains piled with sugar.
Do nothing and don't squeeze the sugar cane.

What need is there for Egypt's sugar
when Shams-e Tabrizi
pours two hundred sweets
into his sugar-pouring words?

ghazal 1140

Look

Seeing the beloved and the world with clarity.

Why are you a dry branch? Look at the beloved's face.
Why are you a yellow leaf? Look at the new spring.

Enter the assembly of *qalandars,* for that is prudent.
Look at the wine, the beauty, and countless *Saqis.*

Know that love is a restless world and, in it,
look at the thousand restless, lifeless lovers.

When you reach that king, whose name I will not say,
swear on his kingship
that you will look at him in a way that befits a king.

When you apply the collyrium to your eyes,
again turn your face this way
and look at this world full of dust and smoke.

The endlessly compounded smoke – what is it? It is this sky.
The dust brings out colours to say, "Look at the greenery."

Don't look at the sun only when it shines.
Look at it at dusk, sallow and ashamed.

The moon, too, fills its basket while begging for fifteen days.
Look at it after fifteen days, small and thin.

Come to the sea of charm, towards the mine of union.
Look at the two drunken eyes of the friend of the cave.[*]

When the Holy One kissed his horse's shoe,
the horseshoe cried, "Look at this state of affairs!"

Unless the patience of Shams-e Tabrizi forgives it,
look at the soul feeling ashamed before such a beloved.

ghazal 1143

[*] Abū Bakr, the Prophet Muhammad's friend, who stayed in the cave with him while they were fleeing from enemies.

PATH OF THE HEART

The philosophical everyman, always asking questions.

Someone asked,
"Are good and bad by Him or us?"
He is still wondering about that –
look at his beard!
Strange!
Although his black beard has turned white
he is still like a child!

I'll tell you why he keeps asking
such childish questions –
he has not yet become topsy-turvy in love.

With four legs and two
he has been around the world,
but has not yet dived
into the depths of the sea.

He assumes he has improved
but, like one with consumption,
he is getting worse.
His reasoning, stubbornness,
and quarrelling have increased.
He lacks knowledge of his soul
and the reason for its joy.

The path of argument is filled
with stubbornness, reasoning, and objection.
The path of the heart is joy,
seeing the truth, sugar, and nectar.

ghazal 1148

Royal Remedy

Persian poets sometimes borrow a line from another poet and weave their own magic around it. Here, the first stanza is by the twelfth-century mystic, Sanā'i.

Under this whirling dome
people are blind
yet there is so much to see.

Bear his oppression,
for the heart's confusion
is the light of your eyes,
O you who have eyes.

I wholeheartedly welcome
this sorrow of separation –
this pain is the royal remedy for
having no audience with you.

The garden of the soul
is joyful with stoning.
We want no raindrops!
Let it rain stones!

Shams-e Tabriz is the pearl of love.
Never consider that pearl inferior.

ghazal 1164

Don't Teach

Learn how to be a good human being.

Don't teach the eyes of the sheikh how to see.
Don't teach the heavenly spheres how to steer.

Don't think the whole is the sum of these parts.
Don't teach the rose to be graceful and laugh.

Open your eyes to see the moonlight.
Don't teach the moon how to cast light.

Watch over your wisdom when drinking wine.
Don't teach wine how to steal your wisdom.

Teach the falcon of your wisdom how to hunt.
Don't teach it to fly in vain.

Make those orphaned by separation laugh.
Don't teach them how to lament.

Make the heart of the innocent free from fear.
Don't teach that heart how to tremble.

Don't let the merciless justify themselves.
Don't teach the quarrelsome how to fight.

Keep your tongue veiled, as you do your heart.
Don't teach the tongue how to rend the veil.

Open your eyes to true meaning.
Don't teach them to gather words like ears.

ghazal 1182

The Sound that Frees Wisdom

Asking God to play more gently.

Hear the sound of His music played in my chest.
My ruined heart begins to throb as it starts.

He took off His hat and picked up the rebec.
When I saw Him do that, I lost my heart.

From His playing,
my heart whirls like a spinning wheel.
The wheel is visible,
but the spinner is hidden from all eyes.

Play a few strings with lighter notes
than those you've played so far,
for those songs are freeing wisdom too fast.

Know that the body is dust
and the soul like wind inside it,
but the actions of the body's dust
tell its tales.

While the dust of the soul is still there
another Soul will arrive,
by whose Songs all particles will be dancing.

The world is like an oven
baking multi-coloured bread.
After seeing the Baker,
why would anyone care about the bread or the oven?

Samā of the heart
is neither from the chest
nor from outside.
Play it from wherever it is.
May my life be a sacrifice to you.

One night I told my heart teasingly,
"Look at the moon, O heart,
it seems to carry the grace
of His gentle sweetness.

For when the sun hides,
He replaces it with a small lamp
to give light at night!"

Then my heart closed its eyes
with both hands –
it is aware of the King's
amorous gestures and jealousy.

ghazal 1286

The Flute of Love

On the path of love, every barrier becomes a bridge.

If a hangover weakens
the passion of love,
help comes at once
from the morning wine
poured by the *Saqi* of love.

The drum of joy
announces the victory
of the army of lovers,
and the happy news of
'Truly we conquered'*
is played on the oboe of love.

In the mouth of a lover,
poison turns at once to nectar
because of the sugar
flowing every moment
from the flute of love.

If a cloud covers the moon,
it is immediately struck
by the life-giving lightning of love.

Moving through the desert
surrounded by burning hot sand,
you will hear the thundering call
of the water bearer of love.

---

* K 48:1.

O *Saqi*, swear that you will either
pour a cup of wine over the people
or call them to the height and breadth of love.

If the light of Shams-e Tabriz
shines through the dome of God's jealousy,
in that moment, waves like domes
will rise from the sea of love.

ghazal 1308

The Calamity of Love

Give up the boat of wisdom and drown in the sea of love.

Again – from the mountain of Qāf
came the phoenix of love.

Again – from the soul
came the cry and clamour of love.

Again – love's head emerged
like a surfacing whale
to wreck the boat of wisdom
on the sea of love.

Faqr has opened its chest
towards pure hearts.
Inside the belly of Mount Sinai,*
see the divine light of love.

The birds of lovers' hearts
spread new wings†
and, in the cages of their chests,
found the vast world of love.

Every moment
the beloved brings gifts
to lovers who work.
He is the soul
who enlivens the heart of love.

---

*Where Moses prayed and received the Ten Commandments. A Sufi allegory alluding to an established, intense state of concentration – like a mountain.
† A new level of inner consciousness.

Wisdom was a problem solver
but retreated to sit in a corner.
Now look –
the calamity of love is everywhere!

Wisdom saw a fire and said, "It is love!"
But no, love can be seen
only by the open eyes of love.

Love called loudly with a gentle Sound,
"O heart, fly up!
Look at the height of love!"

Look at Shams-e Din,
king of the people of Tabriz,
joy of pure souls
and the eyes of hearts in love.

ghazal 1311

God's Workshop

God is visible inside the heart.

What a workshop You have inside this heart!
What idols[*] You paint inside this heart!

Spring has come, it's time to sow.
Who knows what You will sow inside this heart!

Outside, You've covered Yourself with a veil of glory,
still You are clearly visible inside this heart.

When the seeker's feet sink into water and mud,
You tend to him inside this heart.

If the heart were not superior to the heavens,
the moon would not be riding inside this heart.

If the heart were not a majestic city,
You would not be ruling inside this heart.

The heart is a strange thicket, O Soul,
for You are the chief hunter inside this heart.

A thousand waves swell from the ocean of the heart
when You bring jewels inside this heart.

I'll keep quiet, because thoughts can't contain
all the attributes of the heart inside this heart.

ghazal 1342

[*] Symbolizes various desires and wants of the heart.

SHEATH OF UNDERSTANDING

Before his death, Rumi appointed Hosām al-Din as his successor. Rumi's followers complained to his son, Sultan Valad, that he should have been given that position. Valad replied that he could see that Hosām's blessed form had become like a beehive where spirits were coming and going. He said, "It has become a place of divine light with the constant presence of divine beings. I would feel ashamed to have a position higher than his." He noted that his father appointed Hosām as his successor and had composed many lines of poetry about him including these. [151]

O you with me yet hidden like a heart,
I am greeting you from my heart.
You are the Kabah and wherever I go,
I am aiming for your station.

You are with me wherever you are,
you are watching me from afar.
At night, when I remember your name,
the house is filled with light.

Sometimes like a familiar falcon,
I alight on your hand.
Sometimes like a pigeon,
I fly towards your roof.

If you are absent, why are you
hurting my heart every moment?
And if you are present,
why have I set a trap for you in my heart?

Your body may be far, but there is a window
between my heart and yours.
Like the moon, I am sending you messages
through that hidden window.

O Sun, you are sending us light from afar.
O you, the soul of all who are separated from you,
I am making my soul your devoted servant.

I am here with you,
polishing the mirror of my heart
and fashioning my ears
into a book of your words full of grace.

With your intelligence
and your heart full of fervour,
what value are these words to your ears?
I am describing your ordinary qualities
because you are me.

O heart, didn't the beloved tell you
in all that was happening,
"As much as you are emptying yourself,
I am filling you with myself?"

O Remedy, watch me –
the maker of remedies – and wonder!
From all these forms,
look at what I am turning you into now.

Sometimes straight like *alif,*[*]
sometimes bent like other letters,
one minute you're being cooked
and the next I am leaving you raw.

Even if you live for years,
you are like a marble in my hand.
I am taming you with whatever
you are trying to tame!

O King Hosām al-Din Hassan,
tell the beloved that I am turning my soul
into a sheath of understanding
for the sake of your sword.[†]

ghazal 1377

[*] The first letter of the Arabic and Persian alphabet, shaped like an upright straight line.

[†] A pun on *Hosām,* which means "sword."

THE ESSENCE OF NEARNESS

Rumi remade.

I was trying hard to become
a mirror of goodness,
but you commanded that I become
a tavern of potent Wine!

I became a tavern for special ones,
became a sea for divers,
became a sun without flaw,
and became a physician
for the ailment of doubt.

You created angels
superior to water and clay.
Then You threw me far enough away
to make me become the essence of nearness.

You made me like Harut,*
then taught me all the tricks.
You were burning me
so I would become a candle in the dark.

A Turk is just a Turk, a Tajik just a Tajik,
but sometimes I am a Turk for an hour
and the next minute a Tajik.

*A reference to the fire of passion. One of two angels said to have been suspended head-down in a well in Babylon, as punishment for being seduced by mortal women.

Sometimes I am a crown for the king,
sometimes a devil's trick,
sometimes agile wisdom,
and sometimes a helpless child.

I shed the blood of the self
and mixed myself with a Joseph.*
Inside,† I am plump and rosy.
Outside,‡ I am very thin.

ghazal 1385

---

* The *murshid*.

† Literally, "face," a metaphor for the inner light.

‡ Literally, "hair," a metaphor for the creation.

This Harp-like Heart

Disciplining the mind through constant repetition is characterized by the playing of the rebec.

I long for him – long may he live!
A ring of slavery in my ear,
I am in love,
I am beating the drum of fidelity to him.

I have broken away from heart and life
and am sitting on the road
to plunder my caravan of thought
for the sake of meeting him.

Except for his servants of sorrow
or his messengers with soothing balm,
whatever emerges,
I will strike at its head and feet.

Holding the pick in my hand,
I pluck three strings at a time
on this drunken, ruined, stupefied,
harp-like heart.

This heart bought a pearl
from the depths of the heavenly pool
but fell asleep without paying –
now it's paying through my playing.

When it sleeps at night, I pull its ear.
When it prays at dawn, I hit it.

How can it ever relish my whip
when it thinks my hitting will destroy it?

If moon or sky, wisdom or angel,
become a veil over my heart,
instantly I slap it on the nape of its neck!

I said, "You are throwing my crystal heart on stone!"
He said, "Because it bragged about love,
I am striking it with the sword of affliction.

Every string of this rebec* has a new moan,
a new melody, so by that melody,
your heart can tell where I'm hitting it.

In each one of its cries, I mix a little zest
so you don't assume I am mistaken
or hitting it carelessly.

In their fury, kings strike with mace and dagger,
but I am killing generously, striking as a favour.

I play so very subtly that eyes cannot follow.
I am playing on the heart that longs for me,
in harmony with its desire.

Remain silent while I play,
for those are not true melodies.
This music is played your way.
I am playing it just for you."

ghazal 1405

---

* A stringed instrument.

Beautiful Idol

Reflecting on his condition, Rumi realizes that it is Shams' effort that drives him.

I have never seen
such an angry and sour face,
yet so sweet!
I am mad from his spells
and drunk from his tales.

O dear one,
I've seen many idols
but none as beautiful as you!
You are my family, part of me,
so now I take refuge with myself.*

You know
how distressed I was every night
but, O generous one,
at this moment,
out of bewilderment
I'm in a different state.

Take my heart,
take it out of this state!
For though I am dust,
I will rise above it with your effort.

ghazal 1416

* In Persian, the word for "myself" means "my relations as well as myself." When he says he will take refuge in himself, he means he has become Shams.

A Buried Treasure

Aflāki tells us that some who came to visit Rumi on his deathbed wished for him a complete recovery. In response, Rumi said, "'May God heal you' is now applicable to you … only a garment of poetry is left between this lover and the Beloved; wouldn't you prefer that the garment be removed to let the light unite with the Light?

"Even if your dress is fashioned
from the finest silk of Shūshtar,
an amorous embrace while wearing no dress
is sweeter and better by far.

I have become free from my body and free from thought.
I am strolling in the utmost state of union."

The visitors left, weeping, and Rumi began composing this ghazal.[152]

How can you know what a King
I have as my companion within?
Don't look only at my golden face
for I have feet of iron.*

I turn my face completely
towards that King who brought me here.
My Creator has bestowed
a thousand blessings on me.

Sometimes I am like the sun,
sometimes a sea of pearls.
Inside, the glory of heaven –
outside, the wretchedness of earth.

---

* This image also occurs in the Book of Daniel, the golden soul in a human body.

Inside this worldly jar
I move like a buzzing bee.
Don't listen only to my moaning
for my house is full of honey.

O heart, if you seek us,
rise above the azure sky.
My palace is such a fortress –
its security comes from the Secure.

How fearsome is that wheel-turning Water,
but as the water wheel,
how sweetly I moan for the water.

Because humans, *jinn*, and demons
are all under my command,
don't you know that I am Solomon
with a gem on my signet ring?*

Why should I be withered
when my every pore has blossomed?
Why should I serve a donkey†
when my saddle sits on Burāq?‡

Why should I lag behind the moon
when no scorpion has stung my feet?
Why should I not come out of this well
when the rope I hold is so strong?

---

* The signet ring gave Solomon authority to teach mystical secrets to the *jinn*.
† The human body.
‡ Muhammad's mythical winged horse.

I constructed a dovecote
for the dove of your soul.
O bird of the soul, fly over here
to my hundred fortified towers.

When I move from house to house,*
I am like a ray of sun.
I am ruby, gold, and carnelian,
born from water and clay.

Inside every jewel you see,
try to find another gem
because all particles say,
"Within me is a buried treasure."

"Don't be content with just my beauty,"
says every jewel to you.
"Any light on my forehead
comes from the candle of consciousness."

I will keep quiet
for you don't have the intelligence
to understand.
Don't wiggle your ears –
don't try to deceive me.
I have an eye for intelligence.

ghazal 1426

* Moving from body to body.

NOT THIS, NOT THAT

Rumi in perfect balance, between human and divine.

O good man, who do I look like,
the way I look?
One minute I look like *Parī*,[*]
the next I seek *Parī*.

In the fire of eagerness,
I am concentrated like a candle.
I am the smoke and light,
scattered and concentrated.

When angry, I punish nothing
but the rebec[†] of my heart.
With my pick,[‡] I hurt nothing
but the harp strings of good luck.

I am like milk and sugar,
though in conflict within myself.
When I am a madman,
I shake my chains.

O good man, what kind of bird am I?
Not a partridge or a falcon.
I am not good, not ugly, not this, not that!

---

[*] A heavenly beauty, who is sometimes naughty as well.
[†] Stringed musical instrument, alludes to the many desires (songs) a heart plays.
[‡] His will.

I am not a merchant in a market,
not a nightingale in a rose garden.
O good man, you give me a name
and I will call myself that.

Not a slave or free, not wax or steel.
I've not given my heart to anyone
nor have I taken anyone's heart.

Whether I am good or bad,
it is not me but someone else –
the way that one is pulling me
is the way I must go!

ghazal 1467

Becoming a Story

Brief and poignant, this ghazal bewails the lover's separation from the beloved.

Come,
for I have become mad
from loving you.
If I once was a city,
now I've become a ruin.

Loving you,
I cut myself off
from hearth and home.
I've become a housemate of pain
from loving you.

I won't admit how lazy I was.
I've become manly
from seeing your face.

Because I saw your soul
was akin to mine,
I've become estranged
from my family for you.

I read the stories of lovers
day and night.
Now, I've become a story
from loving you.

ghazal 1499

Enchantment

A sad and simple tale: God has exiled the soul into the material world and the soul laments His command.

I have travelled around
and looked at every town,
but never have I seen a town
like the city of Love.

I did not value that city at first.
I suffered long exiles in ignorance.

Such a sweet land of sugar I left behind.
Like an animal, I grazed on grass of any kind.

Why did I choose, like Moses' followers,
rotten food and onions over manna and quail?*

Unlike love, any sound I heard in the world
was hollow, like the beat of a kettledrum.

The sound of that kettledrum caused my fall
from that eternal world to this mortal one.

As a single pure soul among other souls,
I flew as the heart flies, without wings or feet.

From that Wine, bestower of grace and joy,
I drank like a rose without lips or throat.

---

*Manna and quail were regular food from the hand of God to the Israelites as they wandered in the desert for 40 years. Also K 2:57–61.

Then love cried out, "Oh soul, begin travelling,
for I've created an abode of suffering."

Wailing and weeping while tearing my robe,
I said over and over, "I don't want to go."

Just as I now run from leaving here,
I then shied away from leaving there.

He said, "O soul, go, for wherever you are,
I am closer to you than your jugular vein."*

He charmed me with his magic
and I fell for his enchantment.

His spells can make the whole world quake,
what to say of me, for I am non-existent.

First he led me astray, then sent me on my way.
If I had not been misled, I would have escaped.

I would have told you how to reach there,
but my pen broke when I reached here.

ghazal 1509

* K 50:16.

Lost in Love

The illusion of separation from the beloved has vanished. The refrain "how would I know?" allows the English to mirror the line endings in Persian.

You ask, "To whom do you belong?"
How would I know?
"Why are you so crazy?"
How would I know?

You ask, "As miserable as you are,
how can you tolerate my love?"
How would I know?

You ask when I'm in the waves
of your love's ocean, "Where are you?"
How would I know?

You ask, "Aren't you afraid
to come to the altar
where lovers are sacrificed?"
How would I know?

You ask, "If you've been sacrificed to God,
where is your sign of Godhood?"
How would I know?

You ask, "Beyond light,
what else are you seeking?"
How would I know?

You ask, "If you are a bird of the air,
what's with you and this cage?"
How would I know?

I had a righteous way of life
that is now lost to me
because of that beauty.*
How would I know?

I don't know joy from affliction,
because you are
an extremely sweet affliction!
How would I know?

Suddenly, one night,
Shams-e Tabriz stole from me
one-ness and two-ness.
How would I know?

ghazal 1517

---

* Literally, "that Beauty of Khatā," referring to Shams. Khatā was part of northern China, famous for the beauty of its people.

Wind and Fire

To become truly human – and eventually to become truly divine – we must give up the traits that we mistakenly think make us human.

I saw myself as a thorn,
so I ran towards a rose.
I saw myself as vinegar,
so I blended myself with sugar.

I was a bowlful of poison,
so I reached for an antidote.
I was a cup of dregs,
so I poured myself into
the Water of Life.

I was eyes full of pain,
so I went to Jesus for help.
I saw myself as unripe,
so I clung to someone mature.

I found the dust of love's lane
was the soul's collyrium.
I became as soft as silk*
and sifted that collyrium.

Love says, "You are right,
but don't think you are the doer.
I am the wind and you are the fire.
I am the one who fanned your flame."

ghazal 1586

---

* A pun on poetry (*she'r)* and silk (*sha'r)*.

Waiting on the Road

Vacillating between separation and union, the soul knows it is "not from here" and so it waits – humbly, but restlessly.

Because I sit in the shade
of the tree of paradise in your garden,
I am so full of joy that I need no musician.

I circle the light of the Sun like a shadow.
At times I prostrate before him –
sometimes I stand on my head.

At times I am tall, at times short
like a shadow before the light –
completely a Pharaoh when I exist,
a Moses when I do not.*

I am like a pen
between the fingers of God's command.
At times I am a serpent,
sometimes a staff in Moses' hand.†

Love doesn't need thought
because thought is just a crutch.
Wisdom needs the crutch that means
"I am blind to wisdom."

---

* In Sufi lore, Pharaoh refers to the lower mind, Moses to Godly nature.
† K 7:107.

In need of a sign,
my soul moans with every breath.
Waiting on the road
in need of just one "yes."

Because I am not from here,
I am a stranger here – a stranger.
Because I am restless here,
I must be from somewhere else!

ghazal 1603

The Drum for the King's Falcon

God calls to us.

If you don't want me
to make you lonely and friendless,
to be your lover at every moment
and not leave you alone,
don't let go of the string –
it depends on you.

Oh, don't be deceitful or play deceitfully!
Don't do that – and I won't.

You said, "I'll give you my life,"
but you won't even give me oat bread![*]
You consider me unaware
if I don't punish you.

I have to pull your ear
or your eyes won't open.
I will give you fear,
but I will not despise you.

Your particles will disperse
at the time of your death,
but why would I not
bring them back together?

[*] A low-quality bread.

I am the Creator of day and night.
As they disappear, I bring them back,
so why would I not create consequences
for all your days?

With every breath you take,
resurrection from sorrow to joy happens,
so why would I not appreciate your patience
and make it sweet?

Each person is in love
with their task as I willed it,
so why would I not
attend to the task of punishment?

I will not place you
in the world of wisdom and knowledge
before I have taken you
from the womb of the world,
like a newborn.

The rose garden of wisdom and knowledge
is filled with fresh roses and greenery.
You close your eyes in disagreement
as if saying, "I won't look."

O falcon,
I am the drum for the King's falcon.
Come to this Sound,
before I leave and stop composing ghazals.

ghazal 1640

FOUND

Aflāki tells us about the chief judge in Rum who travelled to Konya to take care of some responsibilities. The judge said, "With God's grace I had finalized the task in hand, and intended to return. A group of high-ranking men who were my friends encouraged me to pay a visit to Rumi. I had heard the stories of the excellence of his qualities, but too many responsibilities prevented me from enjoying his company. Finally, that group of friends and I were able to see him." As they entered the madrasa, Rumi greeted them. The judge said when he looked at Rumi, "I lost my wisdom." Rumi took him aside and said:[153]

O chosen friend,
how have I found you?

O you, my heart and my beloved,
how have I found you?

Every time you run away from our affair
in the midst of your affairs,
how have I found you?

More than once you promised to come,
but it did not happen.
O idol, this time, how have I found you?

How much it costs
to bear the burden of others –
how much!
Without others around,
how have I found you?

O you, who have torn the lovers' veils,
remove the veil now that I have found you!

O you, whose face
shames roses and rose gardens,
in the rose and the rose garden,
how have I found you?

O heart, the wound of the evil eye
is not small.
Do not say repeatedly,
"How have I found you?"

O you, whom kings have not seen
even in their dreams,
it is strange how in wakefulness
I have found you.

The light shines from you, Shams-e Tabrizi.
How, in that light, have I found you?

ghazal 1660

Loosen the Strap

Complete absorption in the beloved.

I became the confidant
of the wayfarers on the path.
I became the companion
of the residents of divinity.

I saw a dome beyond the six directions.
I became dust and carpeted that dome.

I became blood boiling in the veins of love.
I became tears in the eyes of lovers.

Sometimes like Jesus,
I became entirely tongue.*
Sometimes like Mary,
I became a quiet heart.

That which failed for Mary and Jesus –
I became that, too, if you believe me.

With the stab of eternal love,
a hundred times
I became the wound and the remedy.

Every step is taken
in the company of the angel of death.
May my life depart if I ever frown on him.

---

*Because he preached.

Face to face, I fought with death many times
until I became joyous from dying itself.

I loosened the strap of existence completely
until I became secure in the saddle of eternity.

From me, hear the undying sound of a flute,
although I am curved like the back of a harp.

Allah, the knower of all, showed me His face.
I died for Allah and became the knower of all.

The greatest Eid* is Shams-e Tabrizi.
For that Eid, I became the grand sacrifice.

ghazal 1661

* Day of celebration.

No One Like You

The beloved is the only one the lover can see.

We heard from our soul
about your beauty's fame.
Like wind, water, and fire
we run towards your love.

Only hands were cut
from seeing Joseph's beauty.
Look at our life
to see how many things we have cut!*

It is obvious what *qalandars*
and the impoverished possess.
We have submitted our tattered cloak
at your feet.

There are thousands like us
who have given their lives to love,
but we have seen no one like you,
even in our dreams!

Like a four-legged animal drinking water,
when we saw our reflection
we shied away from our self.

ghazal 1701

---

* Detachment from the world.

Merchants Without Merchandise

Steps to love, the ultimate destination.

Give us the wine of equanimity
so we can become concentrated
and chisel away our images, one by one –
to become asleep to ourselves,
colourless as water.

We are branches of the same tree,
all slaves of the same master.
Our nature is like love,
both hidden and manifest –
concealed in the city of love,
revealed in love's lane.

Seeing ourselves as dead,
we sit on our graves.
Seeing ourselves alive, wailing,
we tear at our faces.
Any face that appears
in the mirror of our heart
has a naughty tinge,
for we are mischievous.

We are a school of fish skimming over water.
We scatter this pleasure-loving body of dust over dust.

Seeing the domain of love,
we become the epitome of indigence.
Seeing the currency of love,
we are merchants without merchandise.

ghazal 1702

I Am Angry!

The anger of the abandoned – but who has left whom?

I am that black night, angry at the moon.
I am that naked beggar, angry at the king.

The grace of that Peerless One
was calling me home,
but I made an excuse, angry at the path!

If my idol rebels or sorrow robs me of rest,
I will utter not a sigh, angry at sighing.

Sometimes he lured me with gold,
sometimes with power and glory.
I was safe from gold's temptation
and angry at glory.

I am the iron that fled from the majestic magnet.
I am the straw, angry at that world-attracting amber.

I am a wayward particle,
disobedient to four, five, and six.*
Not just defiant to five and six – angry at Allah!

You can't comprehend this,
because you are outside the water.
If you even resemble the sun,
I am angry at resemblances.

ghazal 1703

* Four elements, five senses, and six directions.

What a Purchase!

The best deal Rumi ever made.

Hush!
Don't utter a word – I bought a hidden treasure.
I paid with my life, but I bought a whole world.

Listen to these words from my goldsmith face,
"I paid a scrap of gold to purchase a mine."

What an arrow hit me from the friend's beautiful eyes!
What a bow I bought from the arch of his eyebrows!

I tell this story to others in a veiled manner, secretly.
I won't tell anyone where I bought it.

Even though once I was tongueless like a fish,
I saw someone with sugary lips and bought a tongue.

Suddenly, I grew like a tree in the middle of the garden.
From that signless garden I bought a sign.

Did I say, "The middle of the garden?"
It has no middle at all, but from the middle of nothing
I bought a middle!

I unified myself with the honour of Tabriz,
Sun of religion, Shams-e Din.
Beyond the two worlds I purchased this union.

ghazal 1707

Wave of Mercy

Rumi liked a certain Amir because of his worldly deeds and his sincerity as a seeker. One day, in his presence, Rumi discussed those who are not completely free of their own existence, but whose talk about non-existence is like that of a man standing at the bottom of a well boasting about his high position. In contrast, those who have become free of their own existence stand on a rooftop shouting about their own unimportance. He compared them to those with garlic in their mouths who talk about musk: there is a difference between the sound of falcons and sparrows, between true and false. Then Rumi said, "Amir, come and smell! If you don't smell His fragrance, remove yourself from us!" He said all desert animals take on the colour of the plants on which they graze and then recited this ghazal.[154]

We will not conform to anyone in this world.
We will make no home under this satin dome.

We are intoxicated, thirsty, and drink a lot.
Everyone has stopped drinking, but we will not stop.

There is a wave of mercy,
but the enemy is like foam and straw.
We will not leave waves of the heart
to be with foam and straw.

In this perishable arena, like Samūd and 'Ād*
we will not make gilded castles or palaces.

---

*Two ancient Arab tribes said to have perished due to their stubbornness and perversity.

We will not create anything in paradise
other than a towering palace of love
like Abraham and Noah.

Our hunting ground is beyond Mount Qāf.
We will not aim to capture dead prey like vultures.

We will not marry the black, filthy demon
who deceives the ignorant
but, rather, the pure heavenly beauty.
In the murky soil of greed,
we will not plant the sapling
whose fruit is infidelity.

Because of the joy we feel
when seeing His purity,
we will not even look at the sacred soul.

Silence!
We will not render the rhyme and arrangement
unless unified about the jealousy
of those not cut from the same cloth.

ghazal 1712

Shadows of My Emperor

Rumi confesses that he may be lazy but he is moving in the right direction.

Even if you don't want me,
I want you with all my life.

If you don't open the door for me,
I will remain at your threshold.

I am like a fish thrown out by a wave.
I want nothing and no refuge but water.

On my own where would I go? I have no desire.
My body, heart, and I are mere shadows of my emperor.

If I am drunk and ruined, my ecstasy is from you.
If I have awareness, my awareness is from you.
If I still have a heart, aren't you the ravisher of my heart?
If I am straw, aren't you my amber?

Aren't I in people's mouths like candy,
because of the unlimited sweetness of your halva lips?

I threw everything of both worlds away from all my sides.
I am sitting beside the 'L' of 'Allah' like an 'A.'*

I don't think of pomp, kingship, and authority –
the wealth of your love is rank and grandeur
enough for me.

---

* Literally, "the H next to the L." In Arabic 'Allah' is written 'Allh'.

I am whole and drowned in purity
like the verse, 'Say God is One,'*
not like the doubtful who are turned upside down
seeing only a semblance of reality.

If sorrow intensified and overwhelmed me,
even so, with love and patience I am ready to serve you.

Even though I am lazy and wake late in the caravan,
at least my sporadic travelling is towards you.

Like a full moon, now rise and complete this poem.
For like the moon in eclipse,
I am trapped beneath the sorrow of separation from you.

ghazal 1728

---

* K 13:16.

Silvery Body

An expression of humility and surrender.

If we fill the earth and the sky with our greetings
and spread a carpet of pure silver for your dogs …
and if every dawn we build a trap for your
arriving phoenix with our soul, heart, and eyes …
and if a thousand pure hearts on every pathway
have a message to give you, written in our blood …
and if only for you we take shelter and make our home
within your fire like pure silver and gold …
then we swear on the pure, flawless Essence
that after all this, we will look everywhere,
anxious to see what else we should do.

Later, it was also decided that we must give ourselves
a bad name – and become bewildered –
and that when the Wine comes for the bewildered,
we must make a hundred thousand goblets
in the glass workshop of our heart.

When the silvery body hugs us tightly,
we will tame the restive colt that is the sky.
When the soul's brain begins to boil in that Wine,
with two strides we will cover the four limits of the world.
When we obtain the ring* from Shams-e Tabrizi,
we will turn a thousand kings and royals into slaves.

ghazal 1731

* The king's ring carries his power.

The Glassmaker of Love

Rumi takes an oath to follow Shams.

I swear on the time when
you called me from the corner of the roof
and nodded your head as a sign to me,
as if saying, "Hello"...
I swear on the time when
you untied your belt, meaning, "I will not go,"
and the moon and I became
the lowliest slaves to your waist...
I swear on the time when
my imaginative heart could not know my thoughts
when I wanted to send a message to you...
I swear on the time when
you told the servant to clean the house of those
with smelly armpits to make room for the noble one...
I swear on the time when
you bit your lip, meaning, "Take the cup,
drink it, and forget the tale of the ripe and the raw"...
I swear on the time when
I saw you and the pen fell from my hand,
with my writing about love still unfinished...
I swear on the time when
you sent contrary ideas to that hoopoe,
saying, "Save your life from this trap"...
I swear on the time when
the circle of *qalandars* drank Wine
on fasting days in the presence of all...
I swear on the time when
they broke a thousand glass cups
but did not break their fast,
for the glassmaker of love made those cups...

Do not drink at night
    like pagans in the month of fasting –
    come to the banquet of Muhammad
    and drink constantly, constantly.

I was in the middle of the talk
    and you smiled, meaning,
    "O simpleton, pull on your reins."

I said, "If you don't sew my lips closed,
    sew the ears of the one
    who is not a true friend."

I swear that you can lawfully shed my blood
    and make my words forbidden to the enemy,
    forbidden.

From meeting Shams-e Tabrizi
    my thoughts see a thousand astonishing forms
    as affirmation.

ghazal 1732

Companion of Love

Beside himself with love and longing, Rumi searches for Shams – perhaps the outer Shams, perhaps the inner beloved.

I swear to love
that for love of bait and snare,
I will travel from Rum to Damascus
a hundred times!

I do not swear
on the lawful or unlawful,*
but on the soul of love
which is beyond them both.

I swear to love
that is gentler than the soul of soul
that for lovers, love is food and drink.

The minds of the jealous
have enveloped the town in tumult.
We have returned from the friend
in a way that makes our enemies happy.

Isn't love fire
and my soul the salamander?†
Isn't love the crucible
and my substance pure gold?

---

* *Halāl* and *harām*, principles of *Sharia* law.

† A mythical attribute of the fire salamander (said to be impervious to fire) because it sometimes emerged from a fire fed with a log in which it had been hibernating.

Isn't love the *Saqi*
and my soul drunk on him
day and night?
Isn't my body a cup
for that eternal Wine?

Cup in hand, love came to me.
Oh, a thousand like me
could be a slave to love – a slave.

My soul and love
have shared a thousand secrets
that no words or talk contain.

Bring immature* wine
because my house is empty.
One in love with pure gold†
is immature in love.

Beyond imagination
I'm a joyful companion of love.
There, we find neither wisdom
nor the burden of bodies.

When love and I lose ourselves in Wine,
that king of Tabriz, Shams-e Din,
will come, saying, "*Salām.*"‡

ghazal 1733

---

* A pun on *pokhteh* (cooked, mature) and *khām* (raw, immature). Immature wine refers to love's difficulty and empty home to complete detachment.
† Refers to the self.
‡ A respectful greeting.

In Praise of Fasting

Paying tribute to fasting both as a practice and as a metaphor for waiting to be filled by the beloved.

Look! What sweetness
hides in an empty stomach!

'The human body is more or less like a harp,'[*]
because no moan, no high or low sound,
can come from a harp with a full belly.[†]

If your brain and stomach
are burned by fasting,
then every moment
a moan comes from your chest
by that burning.

A thousand veils you will burn
every moment by that burning.
A thousand foundations you will erect
with your effort and ambition.

Have an empty stomach
and moan in need like a flute.
Have an empty stomach
and talk of mysteries like a pen.

[*] A hadith.
[†] Before the harp is carved from solid wood.

When your stomach becomes full,
a devil instead of wisdom
and an idol instead of Kabah
will immediately assemble.

When you keep fasting,
virtues gather before you
like servants, attendants, and slaves.

Keep fasting
for that is like Solomon's ring.*
Don't let a demon steal that ring –
don't disturb the realm.

If you lose your realm
and your army runs away,
your army will return,
raising your banner.

To those who were fasting,
heavenly food came from the sky
through the diligent prayers
of Mary and Jesus.

So fast, and wait for generosity's banquet,
because that banquet is far better
than cabbage soup!

ghazal 1739

* The ring that gave him spiritual power.

A Sea Drowned in Itself

Some disciples related that Queen Gorji Khatūn was among Rumi's special devotees. She needed to go to another town because the Sultan did not want to be without her political skills. Not wishing to be away from Rumi, she asked a skilled artist to make a likeness of Rumi's face on his best paper to accompany her on her journey. The artist, with pen in hand, looked closely at Rumi who stood right above him. He drew a beautiful picture of Rumi's face. Then he looked at Rumi again and what he saw was not what he had seen the first time, so he made another image on a new piece of paper. When he finished and looked yet again, he saw another face! In this way, he drew many images and, each time he looked at Rumi, he again saw a different face. He became so very perplexed that he fainted. After regaining consciousness, he broke all his pens![155]

Then Rumi began to compose this ghazal.

Ah, how colourless and signless I am.
When will I see myself the way I am?

You said, "Place mysteries in the middle."
Where is the middle of this middle where I am?

When will this soul of mine be unmoved?
Such an unmoved yet moving one that I am.

My sea drowned in itself –
that strange, wondrous, shoreless sea that I am.

Do not seek me in this world or the other,
for both worlds are lost in that world where I am.

Like non-existence, I am free of loss or gain –
unique with no gain and no loss I am.

I said, "O soul, you are exactly like us."
He said, "What does 'exactly' mean
in this visible state that I am?"

I said, "You are That." He said, "Hey, quiet,
no tongue has uttered that which I am."

I said, "Because it was not spoken by any tongue,
a tongueless speaker is now what I am."

I was moving towards annihilation without feet.
A footless runner is now what I am.

A call came – why do you run?
Look at this apparent yet hidden state that I am.

Once I saw Shams-e Tabrizi,
such a unique sea, treasure, and mine that now I am.

ghazal 1759

Turning Like a Wheel

The transition between being human and becoming God.

How would you know what kind of bird we are –
and what we recite quietly with every breath in our heart?

How can anyone find us?
We are sometimes a treasure, sometimes a ruin.

It is for our sake that the wheel is turning.
That is why we are turning like a wheel.*

Why would we ever linger in this house
when all of us are guests?

Though it appears that we are beggars in this alley,
look at our attributes to see what a king we are!

Tomorrow we will be king of all Egypt,
so there is no sadness if today we are a prisoner.

As long as we are in this form,
we do not hurt others nor are we hurt by them.

Because Shams-e Tabriz is our moon,
we are infinitely more than all we said we are.

ghazal 1767

* The first wheel alludes to the wheel of time, the second to Rumi dancing in *samā*.

I Was Burnt

Rumi writes about the challenges he faced teaching spirituality.

So many hearts' desires have I fulfilled,
so many lights of wisdom I lit!

Such strange turns have I taught
to the old sky who turns without respite.

The treasure of generosity became my guest.
Through generosity, I repaid the mendicants' debts.

The sum of my life is but three words –
I was burnt, I was burnt, I was burnt.

In the likeness of a candle, I risked it all
and let all the gains I'd made flow out.

So many subtle points about the Jesus of the soul
I pushed into the hearts and ears of donkeys.

Stop! If I say too much
Shams* will tell me not to say any more!

ghazal 1768

* Literally, "witty idol."

God in Residence

Once we are aware of the divine within, desire for oneness increases, attachment to the physical declines, and fear of death wanes.

Someone who sees You
yet still treasures his body
sees nothing in the mirror
but the blackness of iron.

I swear on Your essence that he is so far
from Your Water of Life
that his pride won't let him rise
like oil to the top.

When a soul kisses Your feet,
it will lick its lips till resurrection day
from the pleasure of that kiss,
O You, Your face bright as the moon!

I asked my heart, "How are you?"
"Ever increasing," it said,
"because, by God, His form has
taken residence in me."

Having His form in your heart,
yet you have sorrow and pain?
Floating in His Water of Life,
yet still fearful of death?

ghazal 1882

Circle of Lovers

The meaning of love in action – some effort, all grace.

Love is flying to the sky –
 rending a hundred veils with every breath,
 giving up breathing at the first breath,
 giving up walking at the first step,
 paying no attention to this world,
 seeing only what you see within.

I said –
 "O heart, congratulations
  for reaching the circle of lovers,
  for seeing beyond eyesight,
  for running in hearts' alleyways.
 O heart, from where did this breath come?
 O heart, from where did this beating come?
 O bird, speak to me in the language of birds
  for I understand your secret tongue."

The heart said –
 "I was in the workshop until I flew
  to the house of water and clay.
 Then, away from the house of creation,
  I flew to the house of creating creation.
 With my energy spent, I was pulled –
  how can I possibly describe that pull?"

ghazal 1919

Who Are We?

In several different ways, Rumi questions whether the self-absorbed or the enlightened is in a better state.

Who's happier, my dear?
We or you?
Who's more pure?
We or the Essence of the Mine?

We've lost our hearts
to loving ourselves.
We're drunk and amazed
from seeing our own faces.

Who's more drunk?
We or the cup?
Who's cleaner?
We or the heart and soul?

Good man,
look at us and the face of love.
Who's more strange?
We or that?

We are disbelief and love is belief.
Look at belief and disbelief.

Belief and disbelief blended their voices,
singing the same song!

When those who know don't know this talk,
how can it reach those who don't know?

ghazal 1922

Look Again

We need to understand what we really are: a royal falcon on the arm of the king or a caged bird.

O brother, look again –
what kind of bird are you?
If the king trained you himself,
then certainly you are a falcon.*

It's not a game when someone
stops associating with others.
See him peerless with no second,
like God in the world.

Because of that Sun,
of Whom the sun in the sky
fills just one cup,
see all the drops and particles
drunk and dancing.

Receive a kiss from the king
and be the focal point of good luck.
See how fortune favours you
when you drink two sips from his cup.

I said, "O alchemy, show me
how you change copper into gold."
Looking towards the heart's goldsmiths,
he said, "See their strong pincers!"

* A pun on *bāz bīn*, which means "look again" and also "look, here is a falcon."

I asked, "How did you bring
Abraham's birds back to life?"
"Pluck your wings and feathers," he replied,
"and immediately see yourself fly."[*]

I said, "From the beginning,
the birds of our soul were featherless."
He said, "Break the cage and see
the beginning without beginning."

Your breath has no effect
because he is not your friend and confidant.
Open your eyes and, with every breath,
see the confidant – see the confidant!

The few breaths your soul spent
in desire and longing –
see them to be equally effective and alive
as the breath of Jesus at His threshold.[†]

Work on becoming humble as dust.
Stop eating dust!
In the garden, see the grandeur of humble dust.

ghazal 1951

---

[*] K 2:260; God destroyed Abraham's four birds and then brought them back to life. The birds, according to Rumi, are the peacock, the crow, the rooster, and the duck, representing arrogance, desire for longevity, lust, and greed. They are brought back to life as their opposites: humility, desire for divine eternal existence, chastity, and contentment.

[†] Possessing the potential for attaining God.

Beloved Companion

Acknowledging the strength of the constant presence of the beloved.

Who will I fear
when the beloved is with me?
Why would I fear a needle
when Zulfaqār* is with me?

Why would I stay parched
when that stream seeks me?
How could my heart be sad
when that compassionate one is with me?

Why would I suffer bitterness
when I am drowned in halva and sugar?
How could winter touch me
when that fresh spring is with me?

Why would I complain of fever
when Jesus is my healer?
Why would I fear a dog
when the chief hunter is with me?

How could I not go to the feast
when the *Saqi* is pulling me?
Why could I not conquer many realms
when that king is with me?

* 'Alī's jagged sword.

The Wine is bubbling for us
in the royal barrel.
What would the pain of a hangover
have to do with me?

If I fight with destiny
and am broken and shattered,
why would I defend myself
when that beauty is with me?

Drowned in favour and wealth,
blissful in grace and forgiveness,
I sit beside good fortune
and that sweet one is with me.

O disagreeable speaker,
I've had enough of this talk!
Keep quiet or, at least, don't speak to me!

ghazal 2032

Do This

Verse-by-verse instructions to be unrelenting in our pursuit of union with the Lord.

Entering the flame,
the moth said, "Do this."
Burning, it flapped its wings,
meaning, "Do this."

With its congealed wick
and broken neck
the candle told us
gently, gently, "Do this."

The melting wax
endured the burning and
gave itself to the heat and glow,
meaning, "Do this."

If you scatter silver and gold
for worldly profit,
you will not benefit
unless you do this.

Filling the ocean floor with pearls,
the bitter sea sat jealously on them
and said, "Do this."

Abandoning good and bad,
escaping all traps,
the phoenix flew to Mount Qāf,
meaning, "Do this."

Purifying their faces
and tearing their robes,
patiently putting up with thorns,
roses say, "Do this."

The early morning wine
became wisdom's enemy,
abandoned concern for reputation,
then flowed through people's heads,
meaning, "Do this."

The *sornā*[*] became simple and hollow,
opened its nine eyes and
pressed its lips over the player's lips,
meaning, "Do this."

For forty years Adam wept,
pleading for pardon,
a father telling his children,
"Do this."

Learn at last to be patient and quiet.
The hardest stone is quietly weeping,
meaning, "Do this."

Tabriz, behold Shams-e Din –
the light of whose soul
has filled the desert with glory,
meaning, "Do this."

ghazal 2041

[*] A woodwind instrument like an oboe.

Beloved of God

Entirely in praise of Shams, this poem begins with the need to find a guide. When we become pure and silent, all secrets will be revealed.

Sit with lovers
and choose only love.
Don't spend even one breath
with one who's not a lover.

And if the Friend
has veiled Himself in glory,
go see the face
of the one without a veil.

Behold that face
upon which
His signs are visible.
Look at the one
with a sun on his forehead.

The Sun
has been cheek to cheek
with Him so often
that his face checkmates
the moon on earth.

'You we worship'
is found in his tresses.
The amorous gestures of
'Your help we seek'
are in his eyes.*

* Two references to K 1:5.

His body is like a thought
without veins and blood –
all milk and honey,
inside and out.

The Beloved
has taken him to His side so often
that he has lost the smell of dust
and wears the Friend's perfume.

He is morning without dawn,
night without dusk,
essence without direction,
and existence without desire.

When would the sun
ever borrow light
from the sky?
When would a rose
ever borrow fragrance
from jasmine?

Be wordless like a fish
and pure like the sea –
soon you will be entrusted
with the treasure of the pearl.

Whose description is this?
I am whispering in your ear.
Don't tell anyone. It's Shams-e Din,
the honour of Tabriz.

ghazal 2053

VICTORY

Rumi meets Shams within.

An uproar rose from my ruins.
The sky broke in two from my pleas.

Victory arrived at last and the beloved
was moved to consider my plight.

God, O God! How that peerless beloved
inflicts punishment on me!

My heedlessness, crimes, and denial
are transformed into worship and faith
by that alchemy.

He overlooks my errors. He gives alms when I sin.

The radiance of the day I met him
caused hearts of the sea and mountains to boil.

If thoughts of others had not been veiled,
my thoughts would have burned them away.

My drum and banner, joyous shouts and clamour,
caused an earthquake in the army of souls.

At midnight, the horizon burst into flames,
lit by the fire of my meeting with him.*

ghazal 2110

---

*Alludes to Moses and the burning bush. Three references in the Koran (K 20:9–11, K 27:7–8, K 28:29–30) and one in the Torah (Exodus 3:1–6).

Where is His Equal?

In a series of questions Rumi looks for qualities that compare with those of Shams. He fails to find any.

O Lord, where is someone
with a birth sign as auspicious as Yours?*
Where is a place equal to Yours?

Time is a beggar in need of You.
Where is Your need for a cycle or time?

Ask someone who has seen Shams-e Din,
"Where is the trail to the sky?"

Do not enter that Sea
without a command from the Sea.
Where is your guarantee? Aren't you afraid?

If you fall in by mistake, he will forgive you,
so where is the sadness for the one who erred?

When a mirror bows before him,
where is the tarnish of suspicion on that mirror?

He is the arrow, bow, and shield. What did I say?
Where is the bow and arrow on the other side?

When a body receives his gracious look,
where is its equal in the domain of souls?

---

*Literally, "one born at the time of the conjunction of two auspicious stars (*Sāhib Qirān*)."

Except through helplessness, surrender, and *faqr*,
where is there one among all souls
who has been saved by him?

God Himself guards him with His divine jealousy.
Where is there a guard he would fear?

His branding iron burns love
into the forehead of souls.
Where is one soul in the cycle of time
who has not been branded by his love?

You are seeking the exalted ones.
Where are they, but waiting in line to serve him?

No one really laughs unless they eat his saffron.*
Where is a truly joyful one, except from love for his face?

Other than separation from that master of my soul,
where in the world is grief and sorrow
for my life and soul?
Lord Shams-e Din, for God's sake,
where is a mouth worthy to utter his praise?

My soul and tongue have been lost from union with him.
Where is my tongue to explain the dust of Tabriz?

Every quarry or mine is in need of a buyer.
Where is a mine as needless as him?

ghazal 2186

---

*Refers to a belief that saffron stimulates laughter.

Why Do You Deceive Me?

One role of the sheikh is to confuse disciples until they surrender. Shams, particularly, took this as his duty – and here Rumi complains about it.

Why again, O idol, do you deceive me?
Why again, with tricks, do you deceive me?

Every moment, generously, you call me.
Why, O friend, do you deceive me?

You are life – and life cannot be trusted.*
Why, with trust, do you deceive me?

My heart cannot be satiated
even with many Oxus rivers.
Why, with a water bearer, do you deceive me?

Without your moon my eyes are darkened.
Why, with a blind man's cane, do you deceive me?

O friend, prayer is the duty of a devotee.
Why, with prayer, do you deceive me?

The one who yesterday
received your command for safety,
why now, with fear and hope,† do you deceive him?

You said, "We must be content with God's decree."
Why, with the decree, do you deceive me?

---

* Persians say life is disloyal because it doesn't last.
† Two states (*khawf* and *rajā*) experienced by seekers of God.

Because this pain of mine cannot be remedied,
why, with the remedy, do you deceive me?

Because dining alone* is your happy tradition,
why, with an invitation, do you deceive me?

You shattered my harp of joy,
why, with three strings, do you deceive me?

Why do you flatter me without me?
Why, with me, do you deceive me?
O you, my soul stands surrendered and ready to serve.
Why, with the cloak, do you deceive me?

Hush!
Other than you, I want nothing.
Why, with gifts, do you deceive me?

ghazal 2189

---

* Alludes to God as the only existence.

Anger and Pride

A clear warning.

Anger arises entirely from pride.
Purify yourself of anger.
If you don't want anger, abandon pride.
Be humble as dust.

Anger never arises except from the pride of me and mine.
Step on both of them and, with that ladder, reach the sky.

Wherever you see anger, look for pride.
If you are content with these two snakes,
go and become a *zahhāk*.*

If you are appalled by anger and pride,
you will sleep in peace.
But if your heart is happy with them,
you will be sad.

Leave dog-like anger and see the anger of lions.
Once you see that, surrender and become a lamb.

Don't eat anything that causes anger, even if it's sweet.
Eat a morsel from the Uncreated and become His devotee.

Become the butcher of passion. Kill malice and pride.
How long will you sleep with these two dogs? Be vigilant!

ghazal 2198

*A king in *Shahnameh*: a devil kissed his shoulders and a snake grew from each one.

Listen Carefully

In ghazal 2189, Rumi complains about Shams for his tendency to confuse. Here, he promises to do the same. He asks us to listen – silently, patiently – assuring us we will eventually know the truth.

You are in love with me? I'll confuse you.
Listen carefully.

Don't build yourself up. I'll destroy you.
Listen carefully.

If you build two hundred houses like bees and ants,
I'll leave you with no family, no home, no hearth.
Listen carefully.

You want all men and women to become drunk on you?
I'll make you drunk and perplexed.
Listen carefully.

You are like Abraham,* go safely and don't fear the fire.
From fire I'll make a hundred rose gardens for you.
Listen carefully.

Like a fast-spinning mill, I'll make you whirl and turn
even if you're Mount Qāf.
Listen carefully.

If you are a Socrates or a Plato in knowledge,
pomp, and glory, I'll make you ignorant with one look.
Listen carefully.

* Refers to the story of Abraham who emerged unscathed from Nimrod's furnace.

You're like a dead bird in my hand when I'm hunting.
I'm the hunter and I'll make you into a trap for birds.
Listen carefully.

You are sleeping upon a treasure like a snake, O guard.
I'll make you twist and turn like a tired snake.
Listen carefully.

O shell, when you come to our ocean, don't be sad.
I'll make you scatter pearls like oysters.
Listen carefully.

No sword can touch or wound your throat.
I'll sacrifice you like Ishmael.*
Listen carefully.

Hang on to my skirt if you are a sinner,† a sinner.
I'll make you a skirt of light like the moon.
Listen carefully.

I am a phoenix and graciously cast my shadow
on your head. I'll make you a hero – a king.
Listen carefully.

Listen. Read less, stay quiet, and be patient.
Then I'll read for you
and make you the essence of the Koran.
Listen carefully.

ghazal 2204

---

* In Genesis 22:1–14, Abraham was instructed to offer Isaac as a sacrifice. In the Islamic tradition, Ishmael is the name for Isaac.
† Literally, "wet skirt (*tar dāman*)" meaning defiled.

Because of Him

Rumi thanks God for Shams.

One whose heart is happy because of him
will lose his head and feet.
How can a heart not catch fire from him?

You're circling around that pool – you are in love!
You're drowned in that sugar – taste it
with your whole body!

When your pitcher breaks in that love and struggle,
put your lips to the spring and delight in drinking from it.

The honey that bubbles from that barrel
cannot be found in the six directions.
Right now, all six are licking their five fingers![*]

What is that Water that makes a lover,
full of wind and fire, so desirous
that he becomes like a carpet of dust on earth?[†]

Why does the sigh of a lover burn the veil over heaven?
Because that fire and that sigh come from him.

Shams-e Tabriz, for whom my soul wept,
became beautiful, a comfort to my heart,
gentle and happy because of God.

ghazal 2221

[*] A play on six directions and five senses.
[†] A play on the four elements.

Absolute King

Shams – how could Rumi love anyone else?

On the playing field of Oneness,
you are the king of all!
You see us all as naked,
but nobody knows you.

Your jealousy
made Universal Wisdom cross-eyed.
It made Him think he had defeated you!

O lamp and eyes of the universe,
you have become unique in the world,
because you fashioned a hundred worlds
within the mysteries of this world.

O you, in love with your face,
the peacock of spring shows off.

On the tree of the body,
the soul moans like a ringneck dove.

You make the fire like a rose garden for us.*
You make the sea like a ship for us.

Because you filled the world with goodness,
O Shams-e Tabrizi,
from the realm of my soul,
I have drowned out all but my love for you.

ghazal 2368

---

* Refers to Abraham.

TRUE ONENESS

The union of opposites.

Oh, when will my blood
be mixed with the dust of my beloved?
How sweet when our bodies
are mixed with souls.

These shells of our hearts
have such pain in separation.
They are mixed with pearls of pure fidelity.

Day and night water and fire
sit close together.
Grace and might united,
dregs are mixed with the pure.

Union and separation accepted
peace, faith, and faithlessness –
becoming one.
The fragrance of our king's union
is mixed with the breeze of dawn.

The wolf acquired Joseph's character
and lost his wolf-like qualities.
The scent of Joseph's shirt arrived
and mixed with the loss of sight.

Dust left dustiness and lost its murkiness.
Water is mixed with the Light of purity
like that of Wine.

How happy is the day
when the Beloved of all united souls
comes to the festivities drunk
and is mixed with you.

By glances from his drunken eyes
everyone becomes drunk.
The familiar and unfamiliar
are mixed together out of drunkenness.

Thus, by an abundance of wine,
Satan becomes human-like
and his curse is also mixed with superiority.

That eternally closed door
has opened by the key of grace.
The keys of infidelity are mixed with fidelity.

The secret behind Shams-e Din's secret is revealed
so you can see that a true devotee
is mixed with God's attributes.

Oh my God, Shams-e Din,
my talk is so inexpressible, for every word
is mixed with a fiery dragon!

Give me a breath of respite
so I can speak from a little lower level,
for this powerful talk is mixed with grandeur.

Let's talk about lovers of the Lord.
All of their future troubles
are mixed with a hundred thousand graces.

One drop of poison
in thousands of decanters of healing remedies
is like the breath of the Jesus of good luck
mixed with cholera.

The rejected and the valuable
have made a covenant and become one –
the inferior is naturally mixed with the superior.

To the Soul of the soul, life is valueless as dust
even though here, life is mixed with value.

Following that Soul of souls,
souls have become like pearls.
The copper of the soul has mixed
with the Soul of soul like alchemy.

The end of the cycle of time
has become one with its beginning.
The beginning of the beginning
is mixed with the end.

Go to the house of good luck –
the Tabriz of purity –
so you can see that this house
is mixed with that house.

ghazal 2371

Become Familiar

God extended an invitation when he sent Shams to Rumi.

O friend,
if you do good deeds,
you will increase your good luck
a hundred times.
Then you can face Us,
so you may become familiar with Us.

I decreased the dust of the way,
I decorated the world,
I disregarded your error,
so you may become familiar with Us.

I birthed you from nothingness,
I placed you on the throne,
I gave you a mirror,
so you may become familiar with Us.

O you, a jewel from My mine,
O you, a follower of My command,
behold my kindness at last,
so you may become familiar with Us.

Become a cup for my drink,
become alien to yourself,
become a housemate of my pain,
so you may become familiar with Us.

O prince, do justice –
free yourself of yourself.
Remember the day of your death,
so you may become familiar with Us.

The phoenix of the soul
will leap out of your body
like an arrow from a bow.
O you, think about it,
so you may become familiar with Us.

O you, who amassed silver and gold,
O you, in love with just any sweet lips,
come and behold Our goodness,
so you may become familiar with Us.

I planted seeds of fidelity,
I drew an unusual image,
I removed many veils,
so you may become familiar with Us.

Trust your religion,
avail yourself of your friends,
love your faith,
so you may become familiar with Us.

The king, Shams-e Tabrizi,
told you to come to Us.
Ignore hypocrisy and falsehood,
so you may become familiar with Us.

ghazal 2436

Untying the Rope

What happens when we finally call out to God.

A wondrous Sound comes
from the sky every moment.
That Sound cannot be heard except
by someone who has risen within.

O you, looking down like a donkey,
don't graze so much on your fodder.
Look up for a moment – maybe you'll see a sign.

The cupbearer has uncorked the barrel
of the sky in this, the end of time.
He has an army of souls
and a banner of pure Wine.

Where is there one lion-hearted enough
to become a lion hunter?
One has to become a generous king
to drink that Wine.

Pitiable are the ears of the senses
that do not hear the Sound of the sky.
Miserable is the tasteless life
that does not get comfort from God.

What happens if, one night,
you finally call out to God
from the depths of your soul?
Leaping out of the grave of the body,
you enter another state.

Untying the rope around your feet,
you fly into the sky.
Like the sky, you will be immune
to misfortune or defeat.

You begin living as soul,
safe and impervious to the sword of death.
You will enter a garden
that autumn cannot plunder.

I'll stay quiet. I'll stay quiet
so love can describe itself –
a beautiful, sweet, and endless description,
nourishing to the soul.

ghazal 2442

BREATH OF ONENESS

The invisible fire of sorrow, the invisible hand, the unstruck music, the colourless wine – all move us towards the inevitability of union with God.

The world burns in sorrow, but is the fire visible? No.
Has anyone seen the face of this magic? No.

The power of His attraction pulls me in every direction.
How strange! Has anyone seen who's pulling me? No.

Samā exists without harp. Wine exists without colour.
Hundreds and hundreds of barrels exist,
but is the Taster visible? No.

Love is a juggler of glass. I am a bottle in his hand.
The bottle shatters underfoot, but is any foot cut? No.

Countless sheikhs and disciples are treading the path.
In the breath of Oneness, does a sheikh or disciple exist? No.

Bāyazīd's shadow was famous and a legend among people.
Was this his essence? No.

Good news, O lovers! The festival of union will come.
Has anyone ever seen the face and form of Eid or Ramadan?*
No.

ghazal 2471

* Islamic religious observances; Rumi is making the point that there are things that exist but have no visible substance.

TIME

The attributes we must cultivate if we are to find our way home: egolessness, patience, and humility.

If knowledge of the ruined tavern
accompanied your every breath,
worldly knowledge and art would be like the wind,
a mere passing fancy to you.

If the unseen Bird cast a shadow on you,
a phoenix in the world would seem like a fly to you.
If the King of Truth appeared to you in all His glory,
the sound of drums would be like tinkling bells to you.

If the dawn of good fortune favoured you,
why would you be in the hands of the watchman?*

If the masters who went before
bestowed their grace on you,
the thought you hold in front of your heart
would move behind it.

If the ear of your heart stopped hearing in reverse,
one word from the book of lovers
would be enough for you.

If the confused one became someone,
he would not say, "All have died, no one has returned,"
because he would see they have returned.

---

* Literally, "how would your beard and skirt be in the hands of the watchman?" The line means, "how would you be in the prison of the physical world where the mind dominates the soul?"

If you obtained immortality, the flame of your life
that flickers from death would not flicker.

If your greedy nature were not in the company of inferiors,
this drink* would feel like a thorn in your throat.

If the child that is your wisdom had attained the blessed state,
why would he be cheerless in the school of joy?

If now were the time, the pretender would be the saviour.
Quiet! Everything is pawned to time.

ghazal 2625

*The world.

Pain as Remedy

We cannot see all that we will have to endure on the spiritual journey but, in the end, the pain and struggle are worth it. Only gratitude remains.

It's like this – and the town crier agrees –
without pain you will gain no happiness.

What pains you have endured
every day since the day you were born –
think about that.

How much blood has flowed
from hearts and eyes
since the day you first opened your eyes
to the world!

O God, if iron knew from the start
the struggles You meant to give it!

In fear and dread,
it would have been like water –
would have melted away
and refused to become solid.

But you hid those struggles from iron
and gave them every day, bit by bit.

When at last iron became mirror,
it exclaimed, "O thank you, my King, my Guide!"

ghazal 2680

The Secret of Harmony

Agree, accept, flow – then join the gathering of lovers.

Agree with the friend as much as you can
so you don't remain lonely and sad.

You will find access to the Water of Life
when you learn the secret of harmony.

Go, become one with the friend's shadow –
don't show a sign of yourself.

Drink, if you are given a hefty, full cup –
go beyond this arrogance, my soul.

Don't take form anymore, O heart –
be like water and flow.

Taking form comes from being solid –
don't crystallize if you come from the soul's pure Wine.

Enter the heart's gathering and there you will find
pleasure and a heavenly drinking mate.

ghazal 2773

HEART-STEALER

In praise of the sheikh, the inner beloved, and of the power and beauty of God.

Don't you ever ask your own love
how wonderful you are,
what a heart-stealer you are?

If you show your face,
the two worlds will surely collide!
You're the wine, we're the jug.
You're the water, we're the stream.
You're without place or direction,
flowing fully towards us.

How can my heart find You?
How can my eyes see You?
How can words ask the mouth,
"Where are you?"

What did You whisper into the rose's ear
to make her blossom into laughter?
What did You feed the sugar cane's mouth
to make him chew on candy?
What ebullience did You give to Wine?
What nectar did You give to honey?
What intelligence did You give to wisdom
that it has such lofty opinions?

You fashioned the creation
    yet the hearts of its dwellers are troubled.
You make the unpleasant pleasant
    for You are delight
    and make delight more delightful.

You make joy joyful.
You make wonder wondrous.
You make generosity's lips sweet as nectar
    for You are a generous, bountiful giver.

You give comfort to a broken heart
    and wash it clean of misfortune.
You say a sympathetic word
    and that is healing in itself.

You make clouds cry.
You make lightning laugh.
You are a thousand times more
    than we say You are
    for You are a mine of loyalty.

ghazal 2853

Delightful Sugar

This tiny poem is like a drop introducing the ocean. Here is the beloved, dwelling among us.

No sign of humanity remains
in the one who receives news
from the realm of non-existence.

He does not focus his effort on causes
even if they extend from earth to sky.

Someone who is annihilated, obliterated,
will see him through the eyes of truth.

He will see pure Essence
adorned with dazzling attributes,
residing in a living form.

How can you be content
in the company of his form alone?
He has become the Other –
go and truly become the Other!

Hear my gratitude for him –
I swear upon your life and soul
that I have never tasted sugar
so sweet, so delightful!

ghazal 2891

On the Death of Shams

An elegy and lamentation for Shams in which we feel Rumi's unbearable loss. Each stanza conjures an image of the inevitability of death, as though he needs to convince himself that the glory of the world and the light of his life has gone. Note how beautifully this poem is written, even in translation, despite the depth of Rumi's grief.

If my eyes wept as much as this sorrow,
day and night until dawn they would weep.

If the sky knew about this separation,
the sun, moon, and stars would weep.

If the king knew about his dethronement coming,
for his crown, his belt, and himself he would weep.

If the wedding night could see divorce coming,
over kissing and embracing it would weep.

If the ruby wine could see the hangover coming,
over bottle and glassblower it would weep.

If the rose garden were aware of autumn coming,
over its tender branches the rose petals would weep.

If the flying bird knew of the hunt coming,
its wings and feathers would go weak and it would weep.

If Plato's skill had not seduced him,
lamenting over that skill he would weep.

If the vent were aware of the smoke of death coming,
the vent, the wall, and the door would weep.

If a ship knew of the danger coming,
dancing along in the sea it would weep.

If the fire in this crucible were visible,
over their silver and gold the wealthy would weep.

If Rostam were aware of this misery coming,
over battle, attack, and retreat he would weep.

Death is deaf and does not hear wailing
or else, bitterly, it would weep.

Death, the executioner, is heartless,
but even with a heart of stone he would weep.

If death showed its claws,
hands and feet for each other would weep.

If death were present at the time of the struggle,
the mother goat for the lion would weep.

Earth is a mother who eats her own children,
or else at the death of her son she would weep.

If sweet life could foresee its surrender
to the bitterness of death, even sugar would weep.

If the reciter of the Koran knew he was braying,
he'd stop his hee-hawing and would weep.

If the corpse were aware of this shroud coming,
while passing by it would weep.

A newborn baby cries while leaving the womb,
if it were wiser even more it would weep.

But without wisdom the infant can't weep,
or else the cow and donkey also would weep.

If our sweetheart could find a remedy for death,
like rain he would weep.

Seeing the bitterness of death as sweet,
the One who could see all would weep.

For my time is over, what's gone is gone.
Where is the news that over this news would weep?

If the poison arrow that pierces the heart
pierced the shield, the shield would weep.

I am under the earth in such a way
that it would be fitting if this world,
above and below, would weep.

Be silent, not even one can truly see,
but if there were one who could see he would weep.

Shams-e Tabrizi is gone. Where is there someone
who for that glory of humanity would weep?

The inner world found the joy of marriage with him,
but without him these images would weep.

If the world beyond hearing and sight
had sight and hearing, it would weep.

ghazal 2893

Sound of the Flute

Music played in samā, music played in the heart.

Oh, you have triumphed over the world!
Sound of the flute, sound of the flute, sound of the flute.

What is the flute for that beloved with the sweet kiss?
Place of the kiss, place of the kiss, place of the kiss.

That flute without hands and feet took others'
hands and feet, hands and feet, hands and feet.

The flute is an excuse – this isn't the flute's doing.
It's only the sound of that phoenix* wing.
Why all this concealment?
God Himself is pulling lovers of God to God.

We are all beggars, 'God is wealthy.'†
All that a beggar has is given by the Wealthy One.
We are all darkness, 'God is the light.'‡
The rays in this dwelling come from the Sun.

In this abode, shadow mixes with light.
If you want light, come up to the roof.
Sometimes your heart is joyful, sometimes constricted.
If you don't want a constricted heart, leave this tight spot.

ghazal 2902

* A mythical bird, alluding to the perfect *murshid*.
† K 47:38.
‡ K 24:35.

YES

With each question wrapped in a lovely image, Rumi wonders if the beloved will ever come to his rescue.

Will this door finally open? Yes.
Will the silvery-breasted beloved show his face? Yes.

Will our *Saqi* remember the drunkards again
with his wine and cup? Yes.

Will a lovely new spring come to the garden
and will those new shoots bloom? Yes.

Will the rose and the morning glory be together
when the meadow celebrates with greenery? Yes.

Will the thorn-covered, twig-covered expanse of dust
fill with the scent of musk and ambergris? Yes.

Will silver and gold merge together –
his silvery breast and my golden face? Yes.

Will my head, the half-drunken worshipper of thought,
become drunk on that red Wine? Yes.

Will these tearful, mournful eyes
receive light when seeing that sight? Yes.

Will my ears, adorned with his ring of slavery,
wear rings from that goldsmith? Yes.

Will this pagan heart become a believer
 when the beauty of the soul gives an audience? Yes.

Will the Jesus of the soul be free of this donkey
 when the Burāq* of love arrives from the sky? Yes.

Will he be better than a hundred worlds
 when everyone in the world is in one person? Yes.

Will sugar cane and flute reeds grow eternally
 in my heart if I keep quiet? Yes.

ghazal 2910

* Muhammad's horse, which he rode on his night journey (the *mi'rāj*).

ALL IS GIFT AND REWARD

Love as the source of confusion, doubt, and jealousy – all to make us give up the trivial and the worldly.

What tests you put me through, O love!
You are aware of my helplessness, but still you test me!

You translate the enemy's secret
and sow the seed of deception and doubt in his heart.

You yourself set the thicket on fire
and then you cause someone to complain!

It looks as if you have been wronged
so, as if powerless, you raise a tumult and whine.

You are the sun! Who can hurt you?
Up there, you choose whatever you want to do.

You make us jealous of each other
and then cheerfully watch our quarrels.

You give sweet drinks to the *ārifān* today.
You keep ascetics drunk on thoughts of tomorrow.*

You give sorrow to a bird that is thinking of death.
You make nightingales drunk and full of song.

You make crows eager for dung.
You make your own parrot chew on sugar.

---

* Life after death.

You pull this one to the mine and the mountain.
You make that one face the sea.

You pull us to fortune through paths of misfortune.
You punish us for our sins.

In this sea, all is gift and reward.
You give only favour and support.

This is the start – now you tell the end
even though you make us lose our heads and feet!

ghazal 2912

TIMELESS GARDEN

Reminding us that God has planned it all.

Once life was defeated, a gentle soul appeared.
When this world sank, another opened.

Although the blows of a pickaxe
demolished the mine,
the goldsmiths' market is full of gold!

Until you kept quiet,
your thoughts would not collect.
Your heart's mouth opened
when your other mouth closed.

How could thousands of houses be built
if designs were not secretly sketched
in the heart of the architect?

A secret more hidden exists
from which a hundred images are drawn
within the mind of an architect –
or within the hearts of all.

That secret can conquer the world
when the heart is purified.
Then no one will die in No-Place.

O Tabriz, out of grace, implore Shams-e Din
to look at us for a time
from that Garden without time.

ghazal 2957

You Are My Friend

Understanding is all a gift from Shams.

O you,
who have taken away my will,
you are my will!
I am a twig of saffron
and you are my tulip bed.

I say, "Sorrow over you kills me"
and you say, "How dare it!
Doesn't sorrow know
you are my friend?"

I am the meadow and rose garden
burnt by autumn.
You are my spring –
make my garden laugh again!

You say, "You are my harp
and I'm strumming you.
Why are you moaning
when you are by my side?"

I say, "Every thought
gives me a headache!"
You say, "Cut off its head,
you are my jagged sword!"

I hold my head, meaning,
"I have a headache from wine!"
You say, "You have a headache,
but isn't it from my Wine?"

I say, "I swear to God,
I am restless like a turning wheel."
You say, "You're restless,
but aren't you restless for me?"

I thanked your lips and you bit them,
meaning, "Hide that secret
for you are my keeper of secrets."

O nightingale of dawn,
sometime ask me how I am.
You are also alien here –
we are from the same land.

You are a bird of the sky,
not a bird from the dust-laden land.
You are prey to the other world,
but you belong in our meadow.
Non-existent on your own,
existent by the Friend,
are you the light of God
or are you our God?

You are born of water and clay –
you fell into a fire.
Know your gain and loss as one,
for you are in our game of chance.

Here, there is no place for one and two –
who are you and I?
Consider both of us as one,
because you are counted as one of us.

Keep quiet, for every point you make has a life.
Don't give your life to anyone else –
you have already given your life to us.

ghazal 2965

OVEN OF LOVE

Shams is the light of the world. Around Shams, his disciples are candles longing for a spark.

Oh, the world is a sign
of your beauty and goodness.
Its sole purpose is that –
all else is excuse.

If your beauty were not
the focal point of the painter,
what was his intention
in painting a figure or house?

Oh, a hundred thousand candles
sit in hope around your oven of love,
awaiting a spark.

Oh, your lovely curls are shackles
around our necks.
The bird of my soul is nesting
in those ringlets.

You ask, "When will I reach the middle
of that king's assembly?"
That king has no limit
nor does this assembly have a middle.

Whose generosity is this?
Shams-e Din, the glory of Tabriz –
that wealth from which a seed grows into a tree.

ghazal 2973

I Wish You Could Understand

A lament reminding the soul of its origin and its essence.

I wish you could understand yourself for a moment
and recognize your own beautiful face!
Then you wouldn't sleep in the mud like an animal
and could reach bliss in the house of the beautiful.
You keep circling yourself to prove yourself,
but a treasure remains hidden beneath you.

When you belong to the body, you are unaware of the soul.
If you belonged to the soul, you would dwell in the soul.
If you tolerated the good and bad of others,
you would be like that man when you are with him.

If you were a simple soup,
you would have only one taste
and you would boil in just one way,
for you are one cauldron.
If purified while roiling and boiling,
you would rise to the sky like the pure.

You call any thought "my life and my world."
If you abandoned thought,
you would become life and the world.

Stop, your tongue has become a yoke of wisdom.
If you stop, you would be all tongue like perfect wisdom.

Stop, knowledge is what veils Knowledge.
You already understood you are the king.
Who said you are the translator?

ghazal 3003

SEEK

Only a very few can see, and only a very few can provide the real "sugar" – look for them. We have the mine of true wealth within – seek it. We have an ever-filling bag within – open it.

Look within yourself for your lost heart.
Seek your soul's comfort from your beloved.

You can't find the joy of the Unseen's candy in sugar.
Seek that joy from your own lips and teeth.

Don't use your eyes to see those with no sight.
Find one who can see to seek what you want.

They say the Prophet said, "People are mines."
Seek your wealth from your own mine.

Rise from the body's throne and sit on the soul's.
Pass beyond the sky to seek your own star.

That Lightning hit your heart and made it restless.
Seek it from your own tears, pouring like rain.

Your body is like the bag of Abū Hurairah.
Seek all that you desire from your own bag.

O You, absolutely signless,
from whom can I seek Your signs?
Seek me Yourself out of Your own benevolence.

ghazal 3005

TRICKSTER

Rumi's playful description of Shams as a trickster and a complete disaster speaks, in the Persian tradition, to the intimacy of their relationship.

Sometimes you come through the heart,
sometimes you rise through the soul,
sometimes you lean towards separation.
What a calamity and what a trickster you are!

Sometimes you are the beauty of all idols,
sometimes the breaker of idols,
sometimes you are neither this nor that.
What a calamity and what a trickster you are!

Human beings run on their feet,
angels fly on their wings,
they see nothing but helplessness.
What a calamity and what a trickster you are!

When their feet and wings are gone,
when they have given up both,
they will understand you through *faqr*.
What a calamity and what a trickster you are!

Like the joy of drunkenness,
you sit in my eyes
and shut the way to comprehension.
What a calamity and what a trickster you are!

In any heart you choose you run like a thought,
you say it and you hear it.
What a calamity and what a trickster you are!

What wealth and what benefit!
What fire and what smoke!
What a censer and what incense!
What a calamity and what a trickster you are!

Sorrow over you pulls the skirt of a soul
towards the direction of a quarry,
towards that hidden treasure.
What a calamity and what a trickster you are!

Pulling it towards the treasure
detached it from all,
so no one ever saw it again.
What a calamity and what a trickster you are!

What a soul and what rest and joy!
What an ark and what a Noah!
What a blessing and what a conquest!
What a calamity and what a trickster you are!

I ask you, "What is this?"
You say, "My sweet Will.
Silence, silence! Enough of this!"
What a calamity and what a trickster you are!

What do you mean by "your sweet Will," O soul?
Don't laugh at me and don't hurt me!
Show me the way and let me in!
What a calamity and what a trickster you are!

You are the beloved of the whole world
but hidden from all –
hidden and visible like the soul.
What a calamity and what a trickster you are!

You make me boil like a pot,
so don't say, "Quiet! Why do you shout?"
Where is there room for silence and patience?
What a calamity and what a trickster you are!

Boil the pot of my heart,
burn my water and clay,
tear my history, destroy the written lines.
What a calamity and what a trickster you are!

Burn me so I may grow,
so that I recount tales of burning.
My nature is like aloe wood.*
What a calamity and what a trickster you are!

Don't say any more about his message.
Now is the time for his wine cup –
let the cup end the poem.
What a calamity and what a trickster you are!

ghazal 3044

* A rapidly burning wood.

How Are You?

Rumi gives voice to the deep anguish of separation.

O guide of our souls,
how are you dealing with the burden of us?
O you, who can ravish
even the hearts of heart-stealers,
how are you?

With the burden
of our complaining at night
and our moaning at dawn,
O loving moon,
how are you?

O you, who did not sleep,
whose lovely eyes did not rest
because of the watchman's
warning and clanging bells,
how are you?

O you, who are unknown in the sky,
earth is not worthy of you.
O you, who are a world
of charm and attractiveness,
in this world, how are you?

Who can ask the sun,
"How are you circling?"
Who can ask the garden of roses,
"Rose garden, how are you?"

People ask someone with a sallow face,
"What is wrong?"
but no one asks the Judas-tree blossom,
"How are you?"

When an ugly face asks the mirror,
"How are you?"
it answers, "I glow like a lamp, Ugly –
how are you?"

Ugly says,
"I am asking it the wrong way round,
as if the field would ask the sky,
how are you?"

I have opened my mouth, meaning,
"See my dry lips,"
so your wine would ask,
"O mouth, how are you?"

When you ask, "How are you?"
instantly a stream flows
within my life and soul, asking,
"O soul, how are you?"

You compose the rest of this –
my head is heavy,
hung over from your absent lips.
Now ask me,
"O heavy-headed one, how are you?"

ghazal 3077

THE FURNACE OF THE WORLD

In the persona of a heavenly denizen, Rumi sings of the value of being born human, advice we ignore at our own peril.

Between the darkness of sleep
and the light of wakefulness,
appeared to me last night in the dark
a dweller in divinity with a beautiful face
who was perfect wisdom
and the light of awareness personified.

Like the holy spirit,
his form was free from the body's coverings,
like soul and wisdom,
filled with gems and free of malevolence.

He praised me profusely and said,
"O you, caught as you are
in the hellish fire of your nature,
the blossoming rosebush of Gemini
is for your pleasure.

Why do you bow your head
towards the furnace of the world?

The throne of seven heavens is your resting place,
though now you're imprisoned
by the four walls of your temperament.

Don't seek your soul's perfection
through food and sleep like an animal.
You were not born human for such a task.

Avoid evil, because in this ephemeral field,
you will reap what you sow with the sickle of time.

Why chase desire in this world
where you assume losing your pain
gives you lasting comfort?

In truth, this belly will not be filled by your greed,
even if you fill it with all the possessions in the world.

I assume you found what you were looking for,
but what's the use when you will leave it all behind?

The night of your youth is over, O friend,
dawn is waking but you are drunk, asleep,
and unaware of wakefulness."

ghazal 3107

What a Wine!

Once fully absorbed in love for the beloved, there is nothing left to do but enjoy that Wine and laugh in delight.

When love for him becomes restless,
when will it even let you scratch your head?

Is there a task left for you anywhere in the two worlds
after you drink a powerful cup of love?

Wounded by love for him, I became empty like a harp.
Nothing is left of me but crying and moaning.

O harp, how long will you complain about the harpist?
Doesn't he play you? Aren't you by his side?

You use this moaning as camouflage.
Abandon this trick! You have It! You have It!

If you did not pluck that Rose, what is this fragrance?
If you did not drink that Wine, why are you hung over?

Seeing your face, the rose garden of souls laughs with joy.
You are two hundred fresh springs for that garden.

The thought of you is the cup and your love is the Wine.
What a Wine! What a Wine! What a delectable Wine!

O Shams-e Tabriz, no words describe you except –
O God, what a friend, what a beloved you are!

ghazal 3124

Hidden

Inner sound and light bring joy, but the pain of separation ensures the journey ends in union.

I am drunk on Wines that are hidden
and on Flute, Harp, and Drum that are hidden.

With such a heart-stealer who is hidden,
our loyalty must be hidden.

In this drunken state, the years pass by
while my soul's sobbing is hidden.

I said, "For God's sake, O heart, where are You?"
It replied, "Among constellations – and hidden.
On my left is the sun, on my right the moon –
that lovely-faced moon who is hidden."

Jupiter put that moon up for sale.
I paid a price that is hidden.

How can my darkness endure when it's lit
by the power of divinity that is hidden?

Now that my fire is out, why do I still smoulder?
It's a sign of an affliction that is hidden.

Let our souls not be free of that affliction
so they can receive gifts that are hidden.

Shams-e Tabriz cooked a pot of soup.
O Sufis, here is an invitation that is hidden!

ghazal 3149

GOING

On the different ways we leave this world.

O you, who are going away from this world,
joyously from earth to sky you are going.
O you, who have broken out of the cage,
free from shackles you spread your wings –
where are you going?

Take your head out of the shroud and say,
"Away from your homeland, why are you going?"
No, I am wrong – this country was a loan,
so towards your eternal homeland you are going.
Because the invitation and command came from destiny,
following the commander of destiny you are going.

Or because a breeze came from paradise,
following the gatekeeper of contentment you are going.
Or by the manifestation of primordial glory,
restless – without head or feet – you are going.
Or by the radiant beams of God's beauty,
drunk from seeing His face you are going.
Or like dregs from the bottom of the world's barrel,
purified and up to the heights you are going.
Or like the virtues of the silent ones –
quiet, hidden, unseen – you are going.

ghazal 3170

The Liberated Lily

Aflāki explains the sixth verse of this ghazal:

Rumi's disciples said that when Rumi was ready to die, he was asked who would be appointed as his successor. He said, "His Excellency, Hosām al-Din Chelebi, will be our successor." . . . When Hosām al-Din became Rumi's successor, he remained as sheikh for ten years. Aflāki says, "In his ability to follow and observe the conditions of religion and piety, he would win over the angels. . . . Hosām al-Din would expend great effort and sometimes, in his intoxicated state, he would say: If it would not break the heart of the doorkeeper of secrets, I would open all the locks in the world."[156]

With every breath,
I would give a hundred hearts and souls
and I would happily surrender them all.

If my body were dust,
at this moment it would give birth
only to passion, roses, and love.

I am water
for the plantation of sorrow over him.
I am the wind for his harvest.

If not for this sorrow
bellowing in my heart,
I would be like others –
no weeping, no wailing.

If not for the jealousy of my Shirin,
I would be the honour
of two hundred Khusros and Farhāds.*

If it would not break the heart
of the doorkeeper of secrets,
I would open all the locks in the world.

If Hamedān† had not kept me here,
I would be on the road
with that unique one of Baghdad.

Though I am so forgetful
and full of error,
I would remember you
even if I had no memory.

Enough!
The cypress feels jealous
and covets this tongue
for I am the liberated lily.

ghazal 3174

---

* Shirin means sweet and refers to Shams. See the commentary for ghazal 1063 for the story of princess Shirin.

† A town in Iran that alludes to Rumi's responsibilities in life.

Bend Like the Sky

Aflāki tells us that Rumi recounted this story to his son: "Today a monk intended to win over our humility by his humility, and take that abjectness out of our hand. But thank God, that with divine favour and Muhammad's intervention, we were victorious. Because to humble oneself and faqr is a Muslim's heritage coming from the prophet...." Then he recited this ghazal.[157]

You are human, human, human.
Your breath has no effect
because you're not of that Breath.*

Burn humanness fully within yourself.
Be from the other Breath,
if you are a confidant.†

The new moon was small,
then became full.
Unless you become small,
you cannot be free of smallness.

You flee from the good and the bad of others,
but all of that is in you –
you are fleeing from yourself.

Greed is winter, contentment spring.
The world's lush greenery is not winter's gift.

* Essence of God.
† Of God.

Think about something wonderful.
Why think about sorrow?
Hunt elephants and lions if you are a hero.

Fly to the sky like angels
and, if you bow, bend like the sky.

ghazal 3177

LOCATION OF THE GHAZALS

The ghazals in this book are taken from *Kolliyāt-e Shams yā Divān-e Kabir,* the ten-volume set edited and compiled by Badi' al-Zamān Furūzānfar (FF). Volumes nine and ten contain an index to the other eight volumes.

Volume	**Ghazal (FF#)**
I	1–522
II	523–1081
III	1082–1622
IV	1623–2118
V	2119–2614
VI	2615–3106
VII	3107–3229
VIII	robā'ī poems

ENDNOTES

All ghazals from the *Divān-e Shams-e Tabrizi* referenced by number only are from Furūzānfar's edition. *Masnavi* citations are original translations except where noted. Abbreviations are used to indicate the following books:

FFK	*Kolliyāt-e Shams yā Divān-e Kabir,* edited and compiled by Furūzānfar
FFR	*Resāle dar Tahghigh-e-Ahvāl va Zendegāni-ye Molānā Jalal al-Din Mohammad mashhoor be-Molavi* by Furūzānfar
FFZ	*Zendegāni-ye Mowlānā Jalal al-Din Mohammad Mashhūr be-Mowlavi* by Furūzānfar
FSR	*Resāleh Sepahsālār* by Sepahsālār
GST	*Sharh-e Estelāhat-e Tasavof* by Goharin

Forward

1. *Masnavi,* I, line 30
2. ghazal 54

Introduction

3. ghazal 356
4. *Masnavi,* VI, lines 4059-64
5. The Persian title is *Resāle dar Tahghigh-e-Ahvāl va Zendegāni-ye Molānā Jalal al-Din Mohammad mashhoor be-Molavi.*
6. ghazal 427
7. ghazal 1949
8. ghazal 1621 as cited in Gooch, p.183
9. ghazal 436
10. ghazal 1077
11. ghazal 3102
12. Robā'ī 1887
13. Gamard from dar-al-masnavi.org
14. ghazal 34
15. ghazal 1660
16. ghazal 731
17. ghazal 1308
18. ghazal 511
19. ghazal 1095
20. ghazal 1135

21. ghazal 1426
22. ghazal 648
23. ghazal 19
24. Aflāki, Vol. 1, pp.513–14
25. ghazal 2973
26. ghazal 52
27. *Maqālāt*, pp.173–4
28. ghazal 468
29. ghazal 648
30. ghazal 848
31. ghazal 26
32. ghazal 550
33. ghazal 2221
34. ghazal 1731
35. ghazal 2041
36. *Fih-e māfih*, Discourse 2
37. *Masnavi*, VI, lines 3138–9
38. ghazal 463
39. ghazal 34
40. ghazal 2891
41. ghazal 378
42. ghazal 332
43. ghazal 441
44. ghazal 463
45. *Shams-e Tabrizi*, p.82:131–2.
46. ghazal 332
47. ghazal 1286
48. ghazal 1129
49. ghazal 731
50. ghazal 1733
51. ghazal 2902
52. Aflāki, Vol. 1, p.207
53. Aflāki, p.183 and cited in O'Kane on p.114
54. FSR, p.100
55. Sultan Valad as cited in Gooch, pp.85–6
56. Aflāki, p.57 as cited in Lewis, p.108
57. Aflāki, as cited in O'Kane, p.54
58. FFZ, pp.35–44
59. FFZ, p.44
60. Gooch, p.103
61. FFZ, p.44
62. Aflāki, Vol. 1, p.67
63. *Fih-e māfih*, Discourse 23, p.108
64. Aflāki, p.226
65. Aflāki, Vol. 1, p.283
66. ghazal 1603
67. *Masnavi Valadi*, pp.61–2
68. ghazal 248
69. *Maqālāt*, p.219
70. *Maqālāt*, pp.618–9
71. *Maqālāt*, pp.18–9
72. *Divān-i Shams-i Tabriz*, translated by Iraj Anver, Introduction by Mohammad Ali Movahed, p.xxvi
73. *Masnavi*, I, line 119
74. *Maqālāt*, pp.189-90
75. FFR, p.56
76. FSR, p.252
77. *Maqālāt*, p.685
78. *Valad Nāmeh*, p.36
79. *Masnavi*, III, line 3847
80. *Valad Nāmeh*.
81. *Maqālāt*, pp.777–8
82. *Masnavi*, III, line 4398
83. ghazal 1526
84. ghazal 49
85. *Maqālāt*, p.730
86. FF, pp.61–6
87. Gooch, p.123
88. ghazal 3139
89. ghazal 1650
90. *Maqālāt*, pp.773–4
91. FFR, pp.61–6
92. Aflāki, p.121
93. FFR, p.64.
94. *Maqālāt*, p.661
95. Aflāki, Vol. 2, p.658
96. Nicholson, *Masnavi*, III, lines 95–101
97. ghazal 971

98. ghazal 2351
99. *Maqālāt*, pp.300–1
100. ghazal 1364
101. ghazal 1760
102. ghazal 319
103. ghazal 1768
104. FSR, p.134 as cited in Gooch, p.172
105. Robā'ī 533
106. Aflāki, p.700
107. ghazal 807
108. Aflāki, IV, sec. 51, 647 as cited in Gooch, p.179
109. ghazal 1703
110. Bahā Valad in FF, p.82
111. *Maqālāt*, pp.145-9
112. SV, VN in FF, p.86
113. *Fih-e māfih*, Discourse 63
114. ghazal 430
115. FSR, p.143
116. Aflāki, Vol. 1, p.467
117. FFK, Robā'ī 924
118. *Masnavi*, IV, line 2125
119. Aflāki, Vol. 1, p.51
120. Aflāki, pp.490–1
121. Aflāki, Vol. 1, p.224
122. Aflāki, Vol. 1, p.356
123. Aflāki, Vol. 1, pp.296–7
124. Aflāki, Vol. 1, p.245
125. Aflāki, Vol. 1, p.245
126. FSR, pp.131–2
127. Aflāki, Vol. 1, pp.171–2
128. ghazal 2719
129. ghazal 1335
130. Sultan Valad, p.64 as cited in Lewis, p.206
131. Sultan Valad, p.78 as cited in Gooch, p.211
132. ghazal 1210
133. ghazal 2515
134. ghazal 2364
135. FFZ, pp.92–102
136. Aflāki, pp.739–41
137. FSR, p.205
138. FFZ, pp.102–113
139. Aflāki, Vol. 2, p.581 and see the commentary for #1426
140. ghazal 2039 as cited in Gooch, p.295
141. Aflāki, Vol. 1, pp.591–2
142. Sultan Valad, p.121 as cited in Lewis, p.223
143. ghazal 911

Poetry

144. Aflāki as cited in O'Kane, p.103
145. Aflāki as cited in FFK, Vol.1, p.269.
146. GST Vol.3, p.189 and Vol.10, p.171
147. Aflāki as cited in O'Kane, p.92
148. Aflāki, Vol. 1, p.405
149. Shams recalls this in stanza 690 of *Shams-e Tabrizi: Rumi's Perfect Teacher*, p.73
150. Aflāki as cited in O'Kane, pp.204–5
151. Aflāki, Vol. 2, p.786
152. Aflāki as cited in FFK, Vol.3, p.198 and in O'Kane, p.328.
153. Aflāki as cited FFK, Vol. 4, pp.21–2 and in O'Kane, p.111
154. Aflāki as cited in FFK, Vol.4, pp.50–1 and in O'Kane, pp.144–5
155. Aflāki as cited in FFK, Vol.4, pp.79–80 and in O'Kane, pp.244–5
156. Aflāki as cited in FFK, Vol.7, p.49
157. Aflāki, Vol.7, p.51 and in O'Kane, p.210

GLOSSARY

Abraham Known as Ibrahim in the Muslim tradition, Abraham was the first of the patriarchs and is revered by Jews, Christians, and Muslims. According to the Bible, he was the father of the Jews through his son Isaac, and in the Koran he is noted as the ancestor of the Arabs through his son Ishmael. He was thrown into the fire for burning idols in the temple and was saved by God (K 21:52–71). *See also* fire and rose.

Abū Hurairah One of Muhammad's companions who had a bag of dates that was blessed by the Prophet. Thereafter, it fed the entire army. Hurairah estimated that the soldiers had eaten two hundred *wasqs* (a large unit of measure) before they ran out.

alif The first letter of the Arabic and Persian alphabet, shaped like an upright straight line. A Sufi metaphor for the oneness of God.

Ali's sword See Zulfaqār.

amber Fossilized tree resin, yellowish in color, that has an electrostatic charge when rubbed, particularly against woolen cloth. Rumi often employs this irresistible force in relation to straw, which has no choice but to be pulled, metaphorically describing his relationship with Shams.

ārif **(*ārifān*, plural)** A God-realized soul.

āyat Literally, a sign. A verse in the Koran.

Bāyazīd Bastāmī A great Sufi master who lived before Shams' and Rumi's time. Born in Bastām, Iran in 804, he died there at the age of seventy. He is most famous for uttering, "Praised be me; how exalted is my station!" and "Under my cloak there is nothing but

God." Shams pointed out the weaknesses in his sayings but also absolved him, because Bāyazīd was in a state of ecstasy when he spoke these words.

Beloved The internal manifestation of the sheikh. *See also* friend, idol.

birds Typically used as a metaphor for souls in Sufi poetry and literature. For specific references, see falcon, nightingale, owl, parrot, and phoenix.

breeze of dawn A cooling, gentle breeze (in Persian, *sabā*) that blows from the northeast and makes flowers bloom. A metaphor for the life-giving breath of the divine that flows from the spiritual world.

caravan Literally, a camel train. Depending on the context, a metaphor for continuity of the human appearance on earth or the spiritual journey. Rumi sometimes also uses it to describe a train of thought.

checkmate and chess Rumi employs the imagery of the game of chess and chess players to illustrate the even greater understanding required to navigate the intricacies of the divine game of this creation. The *murshid* acquires the knowledge needed to become God's playing partner, ransoms the lovers of God (seekers), and ultimately checkmates the lover's mind to the advantage of the lover.

collyrium An eyeshadow made of herbs and various substances, collyrium is traditionally believed to be imbued with magical properties and is applied to the eyes to improve sight. Used in Sufi poetry as a metaphor for the power of God to bring sight to the spiritually blind.

cupbearer See *Saqi.*

cutting one's hands An expression that denotes being rendered powerless by beauty. *See also* Joseph.

dervish A Muslim *faqir,* who is a seeker of God, humble in both character and means, and fully aware of his state in comparison to God's. A Sufi teacher may sometimes call himself a dervish out of humility. A true dervish is a perfectly God-realized soul.

dome Used to mean the outer and the inner sky. Sometimes referred to as the "whirling dome," "satin dome," "dome of God's jealousy," and "unique dome." *See also* sky.

drunkard In Sufi poetry, a metaphor for the lover or disciple who is drunk on divine love.

drunkenness In Sufi poetry, it describes the state in which love completely takes over a lover's existence, thereby flushing out all ego.

Eid Literally, festival. There are three Eids: Eid-e Nowruz that is celebrated as Persian new year; Eid al-Fitr, the day of the new moon at the end of Ramadan, the obligatory month of fasting; and Eid al-Adhā, the festival of sacrifice at the end of the period of the *Hajj*.

face Used as a Sufi metaphor for God's divine light.

falcon A bird (soul) that longs to return to the arm of the King (Lord). In the *Masnavi,* Rumi twice tells the tale of the falcon who fled from its king to live with an old woman. She clipped its wings, cut its talons, and fed it straw. The king, searching far and wide, eventually found it and wept over the condition of his once-majestic companion. He upbraided the falcon for fleeing and told it that it had made a hell of its paradise because, although it was a falcon, it did not retain its faith in him, the king.

faqr Literally, poverty. One of the most important tenets of Sufism, it refers to the soul's realization of God as the creator, sustainer, and destroyer of existence, hence describes the loss of ego. A well-known hadith from the Prophet Muhammad says, "*Faqr* is my honour and pride." The total annihilation of the self is thus seen as key to the attainment of union with the divine.

Farsi The language spoken in Iran; also called Persian.

fatiha The first passage in the Koran; it is recited several times in each of the five daily prayers and also when someone dies.

fire Referencing the fire of longing, or the burning desire to see the beloved. Can also mean the fire of passion or carnal desire. Rose gardens made from fire reference the iconic story of Abraham and Nimrod: Abraham, having shattered the clay idols that were objects of worship for his people, was cast into a fire on Nimrod's order; God miraculously transformed the life-threatening fire into a beautiful rose garden. *See also* Abraham.

focal point See *qibla*.

friend The sheikh.

ghazal A poetic form consisting of rhyming couplets and a refrain, with each line sharing the same metre. One of the oldest poetic forms, it is often used to express the soul's pain of separation or the beauty of the beloved. A stringent style in the original Farsi, usually rendered more freely in English.

glass The spiritual heart.

good man The philosophical everyman who asks pertinent questions but is trapped into looking for answers only with his mind, a fruitless pursuit.

hadith Literally, saying or narration. Reports of sayings and actions of the Prophet, his companions, and his successors; these form part of Islam's oral tradition. They constitute the major source of guidance for Muslims apart from the Koran.

Hajj The pilgrimage to the Kabah, in Mecca, Saudi Arabia that is considered a mandatory religious duty for Muslims, for those capable of doing so. The Kabah is the most sacred site in Islam, considered to be the "House of God." There are specific rules and regulations that must be observed, Muslims believe, in order for the pilgrimage to be acceptable to God. One who has successfully completed the *Hajj* is called a *hājji*.

Hallāj Husayn ibn Mansur-i Hallāj was one of the most renowned Sufi masters before Shams. He was born around 858 in Bayzā, a town in the state of Fārs in Iran. He pursued his spiritual quest by travelling extensively and staying with different sheikhs. A God lover with an immense desire for oneness with his Beloved, he openly declared, "*Ana al-Haqq*" or "I am the Truth, God," and this statement ultimately proved fatal. Religious clerics and other Sufis convicted him of heresy for this bold and courageous expression of his spiritual attainments and executed him in 922.

halva A dense, sweet confection found throughout the Middle East and Indian subcontinent.

Haqq Truth, God, the uncreated, the Creator. *al-Haqq* is one of the names of God in the Koran.

heart Often refers to the spiritual centre within. In some traditions, the spiritual heart is the focus for meditation, a spot located above and between the eyes.

heathen In Sufi lore, references one in a state of dispersion, one who is scattered after being concentrated, or one who is heedless of God, with a heart inattentive to Truth. A heathen can also mean someone who has not yet gone beyond the level of names, attributes, and actions (which describes an early stage on the Sufi path) and has thus not realized the essence of God. In an alternative context, heathen (*kāfir*), as related to the doctrine of *kufr*, is used to describe a God-realized soul.

hoopoe In Farid al-Din 'Attar's *Conference of the Birds*, the hoopoe is the leader of the birds and refers to the sheikh.

house Kabah (God's house), inner sky, or the human body, depending on the context.

Ibn al-'Arabī Muhy al-Din Muhammad ibn 'Ali al-'Arabī is among the greatest of all Arabic Sufi masters. A contemporary of Shams, he was born in 1165 in Andalusia, Spain at the time of strong Islamic-Arabic influence. He died in 1240, having travelled extensively throughout his life. He is renowned for his many books on mysticism, including *Fusūs al-Hikam*.

idol In Sufi poetry, often identifies the sheikh, remembrance of whom is essential on the path; also seen as the source of all beauty and love.

jinn Genies that can appear in human and animal form.

Joseph Son of Jacob and Biblical prophet; also known as Yūsuf. Famous for his beauty and his ability to interpret dreams, his life is detailed in the Koran and, hence, in Sufi poetry and stories. Joseph symbolizes separation from the beloved, the soul's inherent power and beauty, devotion, trust in God, and chaste character. In one famous incident, women who were peeling fruit became so distracted by his beauty as he walked by that they cut their own hands. Rumi uses "cutting one's hands" as a metaphor for complete absorption in the beloved.

Kabah In Islam, God's house, situated in Mecca, Saudi Arabia. *See also Hajj*, house, and Mecca.

Khizr (Khidhr) A legendary prophet who discovered and drank the water of life and thus became immortal. He acts as guide for those who have lost the way. In one traditional story, God informed Moses that there was someone named Khizr who was more knowledgeable than he, so Moses set out to find and learn from him (K 18:60–82). Although never actually named in the Koran, he occurs in a number of stories that usually include Moses.

Konya The city in Turkey where Rumi spent much of his life.

Koran (Quran) The sacred scripture of Islam. Written in Arabic, it documents the Prophet Muhammad's revelations in the first part of the seventh century (610–632). It consists of 114 chapters covering many different topics – spiritual, ritual worship, legal, social, moral, and scientific. The "K" numbers identify passages from the Koran by chapter and verse.

lion A frequent image in Rumi's poetry, it typically references past prophets, sheikhs, or *murshids*.

madrasa Literally, school. The place where, for instance, Rumi taught Islamic law. Equivalent to a college, an institution that teaches the religious sciences of Islam.

Majnūn The lover of Laila. His original name was Qais, but in his bold and boundless love for Laila he went "mad" and came to be known as Majnūn, the mad one. Mad with love, only his own death put an end to his suffering, and his faithful mistress soon followed.

man Employed by Sufis metaphorically to denote the power, courage, persistence, and perseverance which a person must exhibit to be successful on the path to God. "Man" often denotes a perfect adept. This did not mean, of course, that women could not pursue the path but, because men are generally stronger physically, Sufis used "man" to describe these characteristics.

Mecca The city in Saudi Arabia where the Kabah, Islam's most sacred pilgrimage site, is located. *See also Hajj* and Kabah.

mirror Mirrors were once made from polished iron. Sufis use this term to refer to the spiritual heart of the *murshid* or even the disciple, where God can be seen, depending on the purity of the lover's heart.

moon The beauty of God's light. Can also refer to a stage of the inner journey when the moon becomes visible within. It is in this context that Muhammad is cited as "splitting the moon" on the night journey when he rode his horse, Burāq, in what is known as *mi'rāj*.

Muhammad The Prophet of Islam, born in 570 in Mecca, Saudi Arabia. He was orphaned at an early age and raised by his uncle, who was a trader and head of the Quraysh tribe. In his adolescence, Muhammad travelled to Syria with his uncle and later traded on his own, primarily the routes between the Indian Ocean and Mediterranean Sea. He acquired the nickname of "al-Amin" (trustworthy).

To attain enlightenment, he meditated frequently during a seven-year period in a cave called Hara in Jabal al-Nūr (mountain of light). When he was forty, God revealed the first teachings of the Koran to him during Ramadan, the ninth month of the Arabic year. Two years later, he started proclaiming the necessity of complete surrender to the One God, thus establishing the basis of the religion of Islam. He died in 632. Muslims regard him as God's messenger, the last law-bearer among all the prophets, who restored the monotheistic faith of the Jews and Christians. By the time of his death, most of the Arabian Peninsula had been converted to Islam and the tribes of Arabia were united under this single religion and laws. He is also referred to as Mustafā, the chosen one.

murīd Literally, one who desires; a lover, a devotee, a disciple. For a Sufi, the one who has given up desire for everything but God.

murshid Arabic for guide or teacher. In Sufism, it refers to the sheikh or spiritual guide.

musk and ambergris Fragrances used to symbolize the essence of God. Musk is a pungent scent derived from an internal gland of the musk deer. Ambergris, derived from the stomachs of sperm whales, has an earthy scent and is primarily used in combination with other fragrances to prolong their scent.

nightingale and rose In Sufism, symbolizes lover and beloved. The nightingale longs to be with the rose or in the rose garden.

No-Place The soul's original home. Also called the place of no direction, beyond direction, Nowhere, or non-existence.

ocean God, the Absolute; can also mean existence, depending upon context.

owl In Sufism, symbolizes those with lower desires. Owls were known to live around ruins and were considered inauspicious. A crow is referred to with similarly low or negative connotations.

parrot In Sufism, symbolizes a soul who is unaware of truth but simply repeats what is heard.

pearl The soul or the God-realized, depending on context.

phoenix A mythical bird that lives on Qāf, the highest mountain in the range surrounding the universe. It denotes a God-realized sheikh, and to be in its shadow is a symbol of good luck. Strictly speaking, the phoenix does not exist in Sufi lore but is used in this translation for all references to mythological birds including the *anghā*, Homā, and Simurgh.

pīr Literally, an old man or a man with experience and knowledge. In Sufi lore, *pīr* denotes the perfect adept; Rumi sometimes uses this term to refer to Shams.

Qāf The highest mountain in the range surrounding the universe. In Sufi lore, it denotes the creation. *See also* phoenix.

qalandar A wandering ascetic Sufi who is not attached to any specific order. One who is completely detached, desireless, and often heedless of social rules – a pious rogue; also a title for a saint of the highest degree. *See also dervish.*

qibla Literally, the focal point. The direction towards which Muslims must face in prayer; the focal point is the Kabah (God's house).

In Sufi lore, denotes the one-pointed attention of the lover on the Beloved.

roof As a metaphor, it suggests the human head in almost all of Rumi's poetry.

rose Often a reference to the divine beloved. The "rose garden" is an inner level where the lover's heart opens and expands, receiving favours from the beloved, and can also refer to heaven. A "bouquet of roses" is evidence of spiritual achievement.

ruby A common Sufi metaphor that usually means the *murshid's* lips.

Rum The region in Asia Minor, now Turkey, where Rumi spent most of his life.

Rostam A mighty warrior and a hero in the *Shahnameh* (*The Book of Kings*), an Iranian epic written by the poet Ferdowsi between 977 and 1010. Renowned for his courage and power, he defeated all his enemies.

samā Literally, listening or hearing. In the Sufi tradition, *samā* denotes listening to beautiful music or singing – with or without musical instruments. It can also include dancing. For some, there comes a time when the inner stillness becomes the axis around which the physical body cannot help but dance. Some Sufis (including Shams) believed this practice could speed up enlightenment. *Samā* has specific rules to be observed, and is to be done with total purity of heart and intention, solely concentrated on God.

Saqi Literally, cupbearer; metaphorically, God or the *murshid* who pours the wine of divine love from his own heart into the heart of lovers.

sheikh **(*shaykh*)** Literally, learned man, teacher, professor, old man, chief. It denotes the spiritual teacher or murshid, one who has become perfect in *Sharī'at* (religious law), *Tarīqat* (the path), and *Haqīqat* (the truth). Muhammad, the Prophet of Islam, is considered the first sheikh.

signet ring Represents the power of the king. Rumi sometimes refers to Solomon's signet ring.

six directions Metaphor for the world or creation; up, down, left, right, front, rear.

skirt Seizing or clinging to a skirt is seeking help or protection.

sky Often refers to the inner regions. *See also* dome.

Solomon In the Koran, Solomon is portrayed as a great and wealthy king with power over birds, animals, and genies (*jinn*); he was also a prophet of God. Islamic tradition holds that Solomon had a ring with which he could control genies and animals. In Sufi poetry, Solomon's ability to understand the "language of birds" (K 27:16) symbolizes one who can understand the utterances of an ecstatic mystic or bird (soul) of God.

Sufi A seeker of God, someone who follows a mystical path through the religion of Islam. In that sense, he either is born into a Muslim family or has to accept Islam as his religion.

There are diverse views regarding the etymology, which we present briefly here. Some believe the root of Sufi is the Greek word, *sophia* (wisdom), whereas others say it is *suffah* (a corridor or verandah). There was a verandah at the Prophet's mosque in Medina, where some of his poor followers lived. *Sūf* (wool) is the root according to others, who reason that the Prophet, Jesus, and some ascetics of old wore woollen cloaks. Finally, *safā* (purity, cleanliness) is tenable because the seeker of God must go through extensive mental purification.

Nonetheless, according to *Kashf al-Mahjoob* by Hujwīrī, "No word can supply a root for Sufi, because it means something much greater than any word. To derive one word from another requires them to be homogenous."

sugar The divine nectar. See also the discussion of Rumi's language in *About this Book*.

sun The Arabic word for "sun" is "Shams," so Rumi often refers to the sun in describing Shams. By extension, he often uses it to mean beloved or *murshid*. A source of frequent word play in his poems.

sword of Ali See Zulfaqār.

veils Anything coming between the devotee and God or the lover and the Beloved.

water and clay The human form. Some translations use "water and dust," "dust and straw," and "mud and straw."

Water of Life Divine nectar, the life-giving essence of God.

wine In Sufi poetry, the essence of God or Water of Life.

Zulfaqār (*dhū al-faqār*) The sword of 'Alī ibn Abī Tālib, cousin and son-in-law of Muhammad, had a jagged blade on both sides like a backbone (*faqār*). It is a symbol of death and destruction.

BIBLIOGRAPHY

Aflākī, Shams al-Din Ahmad-e. *Manāqeb al-Ārefin* [The Feats of the Knowers of God]. Translated by John O'Kane. Leiden: Brill, 2002.

———. *Manāqeb al-Ārefīn* [Outstanding Merits of the God-Realized]. 2 vols. Edited by Tahsin Yāziji. Tehran: Donyā-ye Ketāb, 2006.

Chittick, William C. *The Sufi Path of Love: The Spiritual Teachings of Rumi*. Albany, NY: State University of New York Press, 1983.

Furūzānfar, Badi' al-Zamān. *Resāle-ye dar Tahghigh-e-Ahvāl va Zendegāni-ye Molānā Jālal al-Din Mohammad mashhoor be-Molavi*. 2nd ed. Tehran: Tehran University Press, 1954.

———. *Zendegāni-ye Mowlānā Jalal al-Din Mohammad Mashhūr be-Mowlavi* [The Life of Rumi, the Learned]. Tehran: Zavvār, 1997.

Gamard, Ibrahim and A. G. Rawan Farhadi. *The Quatrains of Rumi*. San Rafael, CA: Sufi Dari Books, 2008.

Goharin, Sayyed Sādegh. *Farhang-e loghāt va Ta'birāt-e Masnavi*. 9 vols. Tehran: Zavvār, 1983.

———. *Sharh-e Estelāhāt-e Tasavvof* [Description of Sufi Expressions]. 10 vols. Tehran: Zavvār, 1990–2009.

Gooch, Brad. *Rumi's Secret: The Life of the Sufi Poet of Love*. New York: HarperCollins, 2018.

The Holy Quran. Translation and commentary by A. Yusuf Ali. Maryland, USA: Amana Corp, 1983.

Lewis, Franklin D. *Rumi: Past and Present, East and West: The Life, Teachings and Poetry of Jalal al-Din Rumi*. Oxford: One World, 2000.

Nūrbakhsh, Javād. *Traditions of the Prophet (Hadiths)*. 2 vols. Edited by Jeffrey Rothschild. New York: Khaniqahi-Nematullahi, 1981.

Rumi, Jālal al-Din. *Discourses of Rumi*. Translated by A. J. Arberry. London: John Murray Ltd., 1961.

———.*Divān-e Shams-e Tabrizi*. 10 vols. Edited by Badi' al-Zamān Furūzānfar. Tehran: University of Tehran Press, 1957–1967.

———. *Divān-i kabīr-i kullīyāt-i Shams-i Tabrizi*. Edited by Towfiq H. Sobhani. Tehran: Anjuman-i Āsār va Mafākhir-i Farhangī, 2007.

———. *Fih-e māfih* [*In It What is In It*]. Edited by Badi' al-Zamān Furūzānfar. Tehran: Enteshārāt-e Amir Kabir, 1981.

———. *Kolliyāt-e Shams yā Divān-e Kabir* [A Collection from Shams or his Grand Book of Poetry]. Edited and compiled by Badi' al-Zamān Furūzānfar. 10 vols. Tehran: University of Tehran Press, 1984.

———. *Masnavi Ma'navi* [The Spiritual Couplets]. Edited by Ghavām al-Din Khorramshāhi. Tehran: Ketābkhāneh Melli, 2000.

———. *The Mathnawi of Jalaluddin Rumi*. Translated by Reynold A. Nicholson. Vol. 1–6. London: Luzac & Co., 1930.

———. *Selected Poems from the Divāni Shamsi Tabriz*. Translated by Reynold A. Nicholson. Cambridge: Cambridge University Press, 1977.

Sepahsālār, Faridūn B. Ahmad. *Resāleh dar Manāgheb-e Khodāvandegār* [Treatise on the Outstanding Merits of the Lord (Rumi)]. Edited by Mohammad Ali Movahed and Samad Movahed. Tehran: Nashr-e Kārnāmeh, 2012.

———. *Resāleh Sepahsālār*. Edited by Sa'id Nafisi. Tehran: Eqbāl, 1947.

Sultan-e Valad, Bahā al-Din Mohammad. *Masnavi Valadi*. Edited by Jalal al-Din Homā'ī. Tehran: Eqbāl, 1937.

———. *Valad Nāmeh* [The Book of Valad]. Tehran: Homā, 1997.

Tabrizi, Shams al-Din Mohammad-e. *Maghālāt-e Shams-e Tabrizi* [Spoken words from Shams-e Tabrizi]. Edited by Mohammad Ali Movahed. Tehran: Khārazmi, 1990.

———. *Shams-e Tabrizi: Rumi's Perfect Teacher*. Translated by Farida Maleki. New Delhi: Science of the Soul Research Centre, 2011.

Vaziri, Mostafa. *Rumi and Shams' Silent Rebellion: Parallels with Vedanta, Buddhism, and Shaivism*. New York: Palgrave Macmillan, 2015.

FIRST LINE INDEX

SUBJECT INDEX

BOOKS ON SPIRITUALITY

RSSB TRADITION

Sar Bachan Prose – *Soami Ji Maharaj*
Sar Bachan Poetry – *Soami Ji Maharaj*

Spiritual Letters – *Baba Jaimal Singh*

The Dawn of Light – *Maharaj Sawan Singh*
Discourses on Sant Mat, Volume I – *Maharaj Sawan Singh*
My Submission – *Maharaj Sawan Singh*
Philosophy of the Masters (5 volumes) – *Maharaj Sawan Singh*
Spiritual Gems – *Maharaj Sawan Singh*

Discourses on Sant Mat, Volume II – *Maharaj Jagat Singh*
The Science of the Soul – *Maharaj Jagat Singh*

Die to Live – *Maharaj Charan Singh*
Divine Light – *Maharaj Charan Singh*
Light on Saint John – *Maharaj Charan Singh*
Light on Saint Matthew – *Maharaj Charan Singh*
Light on Sant Mat – *Maharaj Charan Singh*
The Path – *Maharaj Charan Singh*
Quest for Light – *Maharaj Charan Singh*
Spiritual Discourses (2 volumes) – *Maharaj Charan Singh*
Spiritual Heritage – *Maharaj Charan Singh*
Spiritual Perspectives (3 volumes) – *Maharaj Charan Singh*

Call of the Great Master – *Daryai Lal Kapur*
Concepts & Illusions: A Perspective – *Sabina Oberoi*
Essential Sant Mat – *B. Bocking*
from self to Shabd – *Hector Esponda Dubin*
Heaven on Earth – *Daryai Lal Kapur*
Honest Living – *M. F. Singh*
In Search of the Way – *Flora E. Wood*
The Inner Voice – *C. W. Sanders*
Liberation of the Soul – *J. Stanley White*
Life Is Fair: The Law of Cause and Effect – *Brian Hines*

Living Meditation – *Hector Esponda Dubin*
Message Divine – *Shanti Sethi*
The Mystic Philosophy of Sant Mat – *Peter Fripp*
Mysticism: The Spiritual Path – *Lekh Raj Puri*
The Path of the Masters – *Julian P. Johnson*
Radha Soami Teachings – *Lekh Raj Puri*
A Soul's Safari – *Netta Pfeifer*
A Spiritual Primer – *Hector Esponda Dubin*
Treasure beyond Measure – *Shanti Sethi*
A Wake Up Call: Beyond Concepts & Illusions –
Sabina Oberoi and Beverly Chapman
With a Great Master in India – *Julian P. Johnson*
With the Three Masters (3 volumes) – *Rai Sahib Munshi Ram*

MYSTIC TRADITION

Bulleh Shah – *J. R. Puri and T. R. Shangari*
Dadu: The Compassionate Mystic – *K. N. Upadhyaya*
Dariya Sahib: Saint of Bihar – *K. N. Upadhyaya*
Guru Nanak: His Mystic Teachings – *J. R. Puri*
Guru Ravidas: The Philosopher's Stone – *K. N. Upadhyaya*
Jalal al-Din Rumi: Divān-e Shams-e Tabrizi – *Farida Maleki*
Kabir: The Great Mystic – *Isaac A. Ezekiel*
Kabir: The Weaver of God's Name – *V. K. Sethi*
Many Voices, One Song: The Poet Mystics of Maharashtra –
Judith Sankaranarayan
Mira: The Divine Lover – *V. K. Sethi*
Saint Namdev – *J. R. Puri and V. K. Sethi*
Sant Charandas – *T. R. Shangari*
Sant Paltu: His Life and Teachings – *Isaac A. Ezekiel*
Sarmad: Martyr to Love Divine – *Isaac A. Ezekiel*
Shams-e Tabrizi – *Farida Maleki*
Sheikh Farid: The Great Sufi Mystic – *T. R. Shangari*
Sultan Bahu – *J. R. Puri and K. S. Khak*
The Teachings of Goswami Tulsidas – *K. N. Upadhyaya*
Tukaram: The Ceaseless Song of Devotion – *C. Rajwade*
Tulsi Sahib: Saint of Hathras – *J. R. Puri, V. K. Sethi and T. R. Shangari*
Voice of the Heart: Songs of Devotion from the Mystics

MYSTICISM IN WORLD RELIGIONS

Adventure of Faith – *Shraddha Liertz*
The Bhagavad Gita – *K. N. Upadhyaya*
Buddhism: Path to Nirvana – *K. N. Upadhyaya*

The Divine Romance – *John Davidson*
The Essence of Jainism – *K. N. Upadhyaya*
The Gospel of Jesus – *John Davidson*
Gurbani Selections (Volumes I, II)
The Holy Name: Mysticism in Judaism – *Miriam Caravella*
Jap Ji – *T. R. Shangari*
The Mystic Heart of Judaism – *Miriam Caravella*
The Odes of Solomon – *John Davidson*
One Being One – *John Davidson*
Pathways to Liberation: Exploring the Vedic Tradition –
K. Sankaranarayanan
The Prodigal Soul – *John Davidson*
The Song of Songs – *John Davidson*
The Spiritual Guide – *Beverly Chapman, ed.*
Tales of the Mystic East
A Treasury of Mystic Terms, Parts I–III (16 volumes) –
John Davidson, ed.
Yoga and the Bible – *Joseph Leeming*

VEGETARIAN COOKBOOKS

Baking Without Eggs
British Taste
Creative Vegetarian Cooking
The Green Way to Healthy Living
Meals with Vegetables

BOOKS FOR CHILDREN

Flight of the Windrider – *Reagan Word*
The Journey of the Soul – *Victoria Jones*
One Light Many Lamps – *Victoria Jones*
A Room Full of Sweets – *Victoria Jones*

MISCELLANEOUS THEMES

Being Vegetarian – *Rebecca Hammons*
Empower Women: An Awakening – *Leena Chawla*
Equilibrium of Love: Dera Baba Jaimal Singh
A Flower Called Rose

For Internet orders, please visit: *www.rssb.org*

For book orders within India, please write to:
Radha Soami Satsang Beas
BAV Distribution Centre, 5 Guru Ravi Dass Marg
Pusa Road, New Delhi 110 005

CONTACT AND GENERAL INFORMATION

INDIA HEADQUARTERS

The Secretary
Radha Soami Satsang Beas
Dera Baba Jaimal Singh
District Amritsar
Beas, Punjab 143 204, India

ALL OTHER COUNTRIES

Contact information for countries around the world, as well as general information on the spiritual teachings and activities of Radha Soami Satsang Beas, can be found on our official website: *www.rssb.org*

SATSANG VENUES

Details of satsang locations and schedules in countries around the world can be found on our official satsang venues website: *www.satsanginfo.rssb.org*

ONLINE BOOK SALES

Online ordering and direct shipping of RSSB books can be found on our official book sales website: *www.scienceofthesoul.org*

ABOUT THE TRANSLATOR

Born in Tehran in Iran, Farida Maleki was raised in an environment of devout Muslims and the strong influence of a Sufi grandfather. Under the guidance of a living teacher for nearly thirty years, Ms Maleki has followed a spiritual lifestyle in accordance with the timeless teachings of all true teachers of mysticism. She has previously completed three translations from English to Farsi and is currently working on an English translation of selections from the *Masnavi*.

ACKNOWLEDGEMENTS

We offer our gratitude to the many contributors who helped with this labour of love. Our special thanks to Ms Jacqueline Carter, Dr John D. Potter, and Ms Debra Ginsberg as editors; to Mr Muzaffar Ali, Secretary and Executive Director of Rumi Foundation, for his generous contribution of the *Foreword*; and to Dr Frank Vogel, Retired Professor of Islamic Law, Harvard University, USA and Dr Razia Sultana Siddiqui, Retired Professor, Faculty of Education, Kabul University, Afghanistan for their guidance on Muslim culture and their Arabic, Persian, and Sufi insight. In addition, we also wish to acknowledge Ms Susan Friedman, who started this project with the support of our beloved Huzur Maharaj Charan Singh Ji so many years ago.